CARVING SIGNS

THE WOODWORKER'S GUIDE TO CARVING, LETTERING AND GILDING

BY GREG KROCKTA AND ROGER SCHROEDER

FOX BOOKS
Fox Chapel Publishing Co Inc.

Fox Chapel Publishing Co., Inc.
1970 Broad Street
East Petersburg, PA 17520

Publisher: Alan Giagnocavo
Project Editor: Ayleen Stellhorn
Designer: Robert Altland, Altland Design

ISBN# 1-56523-078-7

To order your copy of this book,
please send check or money order
for $24.95 plus $2.50 shipping to:
Fox Books Orders
1970 Broad Street
East Petersburg, PA 17520

Please try your favorite book supplier first!

DEDICATION

Dedicated to our wives, Nanette and Sheila, and to our
parents and friends for their continued love and support

TABLE OF CONTENTS

ABOUT THE AUTHORS

GREG KROCKTA

For nearly two decades, Greg Krockta has been adorning his native Long Island, New York, with hand carved wood signs. He estimates that he has carved, lettered, painted and gold-leafed at least 6,000 signs during that time.

Greg chose sign carving as a career because it gave him an opportunity to be a full-time carver. His work ranges in size from small name plaques to commercial signs that span 50' in length.

Greg is also a sculptor, working in such materials as burls to explore human and animal forms. His sculptures have been featured in *Fine Woodworking*, *Woodshop News* and *Woodcarving Magazine*.

He lives with his wife in Northport, Long Island, New York.

ROGER SCHROEDER

Roger Schroeder's success as a writer began when he failed to write the great American novel. Instead, he turned to writing about his hobby: woodworking. Sharpening his skills and his photography and expanding his interests, he went on to author 12 books and some 80 magazine articles. Ranging in scope from woodcarving to housebuilding, the books include titles such as *How to Carve Wildfowl* and *Timber Frame Construction*.

Despite the prolific output, this has not been Roger's full-time profession. He is a high school English teacher, specializing in teaching writing and research.

When Roger is not teaching, he is lecturing on topics such as how to make wood into furniture, houses and sculpture. In the remaining time he is an amateur cabinetmaker—specializing in Victorian reproductions—and an amateur bird carver who has received a number of blue ribbons for his natural wood sculptures.

Roger lives with his wife in Amityville, Long Island, New York.

INTRODUCTION

No one knows when and where the first wood signs originated. We can only speculate that they came about when man erected wooden dwellings and scratched out a written language. A stone sign found at a tavern in Pompeii shows two slaves carrying a wine jar. It is this connection of tavern and sign that brings us to England where today there are some 14,000 pubs. Most of them have wooden signs that are carved. In fact, sign and pub have become inseparable, and the oldest may date to the ninth century A.D. Centuries later the handcarved sign made its way to colonial New England where it advertised first taverns and then businesses.

Carved signs also became popular owing to sailing ships. In the nineteenth century, sailing vessels were required to display their names. This was the origin of the name board on the ship's stern and the quarterboards, which are name boards on the ship's four quarters, two forward and two aft, port and starboard. These boards quickly became decorated with scrollwork and nautical themes such as shells and dolphins. Some eventually lost their rectangular shape to resemble ribbons with ends that folded on themselves. All forms showed off the skills of the ship carver.

Today the carved wood sign has proliferated across the country where it gives identity to houses and commercial businesses as well as boats.

Still, wood signs are outnumbered by plastic, metal and neon. Despite some deterioration, plastic lasts longer than wood and neon is a brighter beacon than any piece of lumber, no matter how colorfully painted. But, there is a beauty and a sense of permanence, along with the craftsmanship and artistry involved, associated with a carved wooden sign that makes it the first choice among more and more people.

Carving Signs: The Woodworker's Guide to Carving, Lettering and Gilding is a how-to book with a gallery of finished signs to get you inspired. It starts you off with choosing the right wood for your project, explains how to glue up wood if necessary and how to sand it smooth. You will find information on how to choose a lettering style as well as a sign design and how to lay out letters on the signboard.

From layout the book moves on to tools and techniques for carving letters by making incisions into the wood. One specialty knife is all you will need to carve incised letters. Plus, there are helpful tips for carving logos or adding appliques to the sign.

Once the sign is carved, you will need to know how to finish it. Your choices will be paints or stains, but the emphasis will be on gold leafing your incised letters, borders and carvings.

You will need to decide how and where your sign will be installed: will it be mounted on posts, brackets, on a wall? Tools, hardware and installation procedures are all discussed. And there is even advice on keeping that sign, especially if it is mounted outside, looking new.

The final chapter is for the professional sign carver or the carver looking to pursue a career in this field. Strategies for dealing with the customer and pricing the work are included.

We believe that carving your own sign, finishing and mounting it is not out of the question for most people. You will need some planning, some patience, some perseverence and some work space. But when you have completed that first handcarved wooden sign, we're sure that you will want to display it with pride.

Greg Krockta
Roger Schroeder

CHAPTER ONE

CHOOSING THE WOOD

There are over 25,000 species of wood in the world. They have exotic names that range from afrormosia to manzanita to ziricote. They range from feather light to granite hard. They have an amazing array of colors from red to green to blue to white. And many, if not most, have been carved. But when it comes to choosing a wood for sign carving, there are only a handful that you should have to consider. Those few offer a variety of pleasing possibilities for signs.

Redwood is an excellent choice for wood signs because it carves easily and is durable.

REDWOOD, A VERSATILE CHOICE

The redwood is among the largest of trees in the world. Once prevalent during a much warmer world climate millions of years ago, the redwood tree is now confined to only two small areas. One is in China, the other is on the west coast of the United States in a limited area about 40 miles wide and 500 miles long. Having survived the dinosaurs, redwoods can compete in height with a 30-story building and live as long as two millenia. The average redwood measures 40' to 50' in circumference, with the largest having a diameter of 15'! There is evidence that the Chinese explorers of the

1

third century B.C. sighted these titans when they crossed the Pacific Ocean and discovered a new world.

Today, redwood, given its name because of its reddish maroon heartwood, is turned into a wide range of products. It is used for decking, outdoor furniture, paneling and cabinetry. It is also one of the best woods to choose for a handcarved sign.

Wood by its very nature is imperfect. It is an organic material that lacks uniformity. Because of that, it warps, cracks, fades, shrinks and expands, and rots. But the redwood available at lumber yards seems to defy many of the adverse properties, or at least minimizes them. Redwood, for example, resists warping. Warping means that one or more of the edges of the board curve.

WOODS FOR SIGN CARVING: A COMPARATIVE CHART

Wood Type	Advantages	Disadvantages	Price
Redwood	resists warping attractive color easy to carve insect and rot resistant	not readily available dents easily often brittle cracks easily	expensive
Pine	readily available light weight easily carved	tendency to warp sap streaks may affect finish	moderate
Mahogany	minimal shrinking resists warping durable outdoors easily worked attractive color and grain	not readily available difficult to carve with the grain	moderate
Oak	readily available gives impression of strength best displayed indoors	hard to carve tendency to warp	moderate
Teak	colorful grain workable with carving knife very rot resistant	not readily available oils must be removed before gluing or finishing	very expensive
Basswood	good for indoor signs easy to carve takes paint well	not rot resistant	moderate

Redwood is also very durable outdoors. Picnic tables made from it can last decades with little maintenance. It has the ability to shed water like good rain gear. And it is also insect and mold resistant. Termites avoid this wood and mold stays away from it.

What is most advantageous about redwood for the sign carver is that it is easy to carve. Though it is a strong wood, sturdy enough to be used as decking, the wood offers little resistance to a sharp carving tool. And softness is to your advantage when carving. This is not the case for most woods. Even what we consider to be a soft wood like pine can be defiantly hard.

Where can redwood be purchased? It is rare to find it in home centers. Even many lumber yards and building suppliers may not have it in stock. The first place to start looking is in the yellow pages under "lumber." Make some calls and find out who carries it or who can order the wood for you.

Much of the wood is cut so that there is as much straight grain as possible. In fact, you will find that boards are labeled CVG: clear vertical grain. It is important that you ask for clear redwood. This means that the wood will be knot free. Knots are the bane of most woodworkers, including sign carvers.

Another good feature of redwood lumber is that it is available in long lengths: 18' and 20' are not uncommon. Because of its density—averaging less than 25 pounds per cubic foot—long boards are easy to maneuver.

Redwood is not without its disadvantages. The feature that makes for easy carving, its softness, also means that the wood will dent easily. So some care must be taken when handling it throughout the many stages of developing, carving and finishing the sign. Another problem with the wood is that it tends to splinter. You have to be careful when working this wood to avoid pulling up from the surface what may be long and sometimes dangerous splinters. It is also brittle and can crack easily.

What often surprises the first-time purchaser of clear redwood is the cost. It is much more expensive than common pine or cedar and is often in the same price range as fine cabinetwoods such as walnut, mahogany and cherrywood.

Pine also carves with ease, but it is not as durable outdoors as redwood.

Mahogany is a good choice for a sign when you want grain to show. Here a ribbon board sign for a boat is being carved.

AVAILABLE PINE

There are 35 different species of this softwood in the United States. When early settlers arrived here, they came upon pines that soared some 200' in the air and had diameters of 6'. Pine had a vast array of uses in the early days from ships' masts to houses to furniture. In fact, an early Colonial flag pictured a white pine tree as part of its design. Two common species of pine readily available today are eastern white pine and sugar pine.

The biggest advantage of pine is its availability. Nearly all home centers, lumber yards and building suppliers carry it. And it can be purchased in a variety of widths and lengths.

Cost effective, light in weight, easily worked and carved, and having little if any toxicity (meaning the wood can cause allergic reactions) it is no wonder that it is the preferred wood of sign carvers. However, the pine used by our colonial ancestors—wide boards that were very stable and knot-free—is no longer available. Today's pine is several growths removed from that. It is certainly usable but lacks the great quality of the old-growth wood.

When buying pine, it is best to ask for No. 1 common and better or No. 2 common. This is a grading system that will provide you with boards that have fewer knots. Of course, you can purchase knot-free or clear pine. But the cost will have you thinking that you are purchasing clear redwood. For small signs, ones that measure two feet or under, you can find pine boards that do have a span of knot-free wood. Or you can choose a length where the knots are minimal and your layout will not have knots running through it.

A disadvantage of pine is that the wood has a tendency to warp. This is especially likely across the face of the board, producing a cupped appearance if viewed from the end. There may also be sap streaks in the board, which will affect the finish. The biggest problem for sign carvers is that the wood is not rot resistant. This means that a pine sign placed outdoors will have to be thoroughly sealed with paint or varnish.

MAHOGANY, THE CABINETMAKER'S FAVORITE

This is one of those cherished woods that brought cabinetmaking in England to new heights. When explorers came to the New World, they found mahogany trees of considerable height and girth. Though it also grows in Africa, the preferred mahogany came from the West Indies and, in particular, Cuba.

The Spanish colonists used the New World mahogany for

shipbuilding. But it was the English who brought it home where it became associated with names like Thomas Chippendale, cabinetmakers who found that crisp carving was easily worked in mahogany.

The advantages of mahogany are several. First, it is very stable. This means that there is little shrinkage and, as a result, little warping. It is also very strong. And it is durable outdoors. Many boats are fitted with mahogany woodwork for that reason. Also, the wood works fairly easily with handtools, an obvious advantage to the sign carver. Its biggest advantage may be in its appearance. It is an attractive wood, rich in reddish browns, with a pleasing grain. For a sign that forgoes the paint to let the natural beauty of the wood through, mahogany is an ideal choice.

Oak is a possible choice for a sign, especially if it is to be displayed indoors. A disadvantage is that it is very difficult to carve.

Many people consider this wood to be very expensive. In fact, it is often less than the price of clear redwood. Where can it be obtained? Like redwood, it will not be readily available in home centers, but there are a large number of hardwood lumber yards around the country that sell not only domestic hardwoods such as oak, walnut and cherry, but also mahogany. Since it is used by boatbuilders, mahogany should be more prevalent along the seaboards. Many of these same hardwood lumber companies will ship to you. Check any woodworking magazine for a source of wood dealers and suppliers.

Teak is an excellent choice for boat signs. The wood is exceptionally durable outdoors.

A problem to watch out for is that the mahogany you buy may not be a true mahogany. Called Philippine mahogany or luan, the substitute has never been the choice wood of fine cabinetmakers. But it has been called the boatbuilder's wood, and it is used for interior finish work. It tends to be a tough wood, hard to work with handtools, and not as stable as true mahogany, and often has worm holes.

ROBUST OAK

There are over 60 species of oaks growing in North America, making it the most abundant of hardwoods on the continent. In Britain, it has been the wood associated with stength and durability. In the colonies, oak gave endurance to what have been called the cathedrals of America—its great barns; and it was used to build warships such as the *U.S.S. Constitution*.

Oak, then, gives the appearance of strength, whether as part of a building, a piece of furniture or a sign. Hardwood lumber yards invariably stock it, many home centers carry it, and it will probably cost less than clear redwood.

Oaks are generally divided into two categories: red and white oak. The variety you will most likely find is the red oak, commonly used for furniture making. The white oak is the wood preferred by boatbuilders. It is no wonder that oak outsells all other hardwoods. But oak is not commonly used by sign carvers because the wood lives up to its reputation for strength by being hard to carve. Oak has to be chopped out with a mallet and chisel before a carving knife can even begin to penetrate the wood. Yet, it can make for an extremely attractive sign because of its rugged grain and coloring. Oak signs, whether from red or white oak, are best displayed indoors since the wood has a tendency to warp.

Exotic Teak

When we think of teak, we probably have visions of elephants moving great logs of the wood. It is one of the strongest, most durable and rot resistant of woods. That makes it ideal for boat decks and trim and garden furniture.

It is teak's beautiful grain, with streaks of golds and umbers and siennas, that makes for attractive signs on the sterns of boats. But the wood has oils which have to be removed before pieces can be glued together or finished. It is also very expensive, averaging three times the price of clear redwood and ten times the price of common pine.

Teak is slightly harder than mahogany but not nearly as hard as oak. And it is workable with just a carving knife.

Basswood, First Among Carvers

Taking the finest of details, basswood has been a favorite among woodcarvers and sculptors. The American Indians carved it into ceremonial masks. Many carvers claim that it is as easy to carve as a bar of soap. Yet much of the wood is turned into crates and boxes, a far cry from the workmanship of seventeenth and eighteenth century English craftsmen who carved highly ornate frames and mantels using basswood.

Very light in weight, basswood has a consistent grain that makes it easy to work with carving tools. But it is a grain that has no prominent features, so staining the wood reveals little of its true character. However, it takes paint very well.

The wood is mentioned here because of its wonderful workability. It is ideal not only for lettering but also for relief carving that can be a feature of your sign. It's big liability in sign carving, however, is its lack of durability. Basswood is not rot resistant. If the wood is not thoroughly sealed and water comes in contact with it, basswood will deteriorate quickly. For an interior sign, it is definitely a wood to be considered.

A Primer on Purchasing Lumber

Woods such as redwood have a nominal and an actual size. That means that a 1x6 (1 by 6) piece of redwood will actually measure $3/4$" thick by $5^1/2$" wide. A 1x8 will measure $3/4$" thick by $7^1/4$" wide. A 2x4 board will measure $1^1/2$" by $3^1/2$". The difference is the result of taking a rough-sawn board and planing down the rough surfaces.

Other species, especially hardwoods, but including softwood species like pine, are designated by quarters. A 1" board is called 4/4 (4 quarter). This means that a board begins in a rough stage that is close to its true thickness of 1"; when it is surfaced it comes out to $3/4$" or $13/16$". Pine is found in thicknesses that have the following designations: $1/2$", 1", 5/4, 6/4, 8/4, 10/4, and 12/4. The 1" board measures $3/4$" thick; the 5/4 board $1^1/8$" thick, the 6/4 board $1^3/8$" thick, and the 8/4 board is $1^3/4$" thick.

Redwood is most commonly found as 1X (one by), or 2X (two by), but 5/4 boards are also available.

The hardwoods mentioned above—mahogany, teak, oak and basswood—have thickness designations identical to those of pine, although the 1" board is called 4/4 and has surfaced dimensions of $3/4$" or $13/16$".

You also need to know that lumber is often measured and priced by a unit called the board foot. The equivalent of a board foot is a board that measures 1" by 12" by 12". This seems easy to deal with until you find out that the pricing for lumber of greater thickness than a board foot increases disproportionately. This means that wood priced at $1.00 dollar a board foot in 4/4 or 1" thickness might be $1.50 a board foot when bought in 8/4 thickness.

Lumber Distortions

Unlike plastic and other inorganic compounds, wood gives us problems because it expands or shrinks continually. These movements are most noticeable during the change of seasons. In winter, especially indoors in a very dry house, wood can shrink considerably. And in the summer in a humid climate it will expand.

There are also internal stresses in trees that are passed on to its dried lumber. These stresses or distortions go by four names: cup, crook, bow, and twist. They can all be seen by sighting your eye from one end down the length of the board. A cup will reveal itself as a

A variety of equipment to protect the eyes, block out noise and filter dust, and paint fumes.

curve across the face of the board. A board may be flat, but have a crook, meaning the edge has a curve. A bow reveals itself as a curve along the surface of the board. And a twist in a board means that on the ends of its length it has turned in opposite directions.

Distortions are most noticeable around knots, which are the remains of limbs. Knots can sometimes be tightly fixed in the wood, but other times they can crumble, fall out and certainly defy carving. They will also show through the thickest of finishes.

When buying lumber, take the time to check over the boards and look for these distortions. Most of them, with the exception of knots, can be corrected with machines such as jointers and thickness planers, tools not usually available to the beginning sign carver. Also, be aware that an absence of problems doesn't mean they will not appear later on. But at least you will not be working from the outset with a handicap.

CAUTIONS AND PRECAUTIONS

Sign carving requires the use of tools, some power, some handheld. Obviously it is best to exercise extreme care when using any tool, especially those that cut. But what we often overlook are the hazards of the woods with which we work.

Though our noses filter out some of the dust we breath and sneezing forces out more dust, there are particles that get trapped in the respiratory tract. Asbestos and coal dust have long been known to cause respiratory problems, but only recently has wood dust been studied as a cause of skin and eye allergies and respiratory ailments. Redwood and cedar, for example, have been found to be the cause of bronchitis and asthma. Teak and mahogany can cause itches and rashes.

Chemicals are also a problem when working with wood. Solvents such as turpentine, mineral spirits and lacquer thinner are skin and respiratory irritants. And in the long run they can be toxic.

The best precautions are to block out and cover up. This means keeping wood dust and chemicals away from your skin. It also means wearing a respirator. Although some prefer a simple dust mask, a good respirator serves the dual function of keeping out harmful vapors and wood particles. When working around woodworking machinery, wear ear protectors for decibel assault. Damaged eardrums may never improve. And put on goggles, even if you wear glasses. Keeping healthy makes woodworking all the more satisfying.

CHAPTER TWO

MAKING THE SIGNBOARD

As a beginner, you will probably have little problem finding a single board that will accommodate your design. A house number or family name sign will almost always fit on an available board. But if you advance or move on to bigger projects, you may need to join up two or more boards. You will also have to deal with imperfections found in the lumber. And you will need to know about sanding the wood.

RIPPING

Ripping in woodworking is the cutting of a board along its length. It has a three-fold purpose. First it helps you achieve perfectly

The table saw is the perfect tool for ripping boards that need to be joined or removing damaged edges.

parallel edges. This makes it possible for one board to be joined or butted to another in order to make a larger panel of wood. Second, it removes imperfections. And third, it will eliminate cracks.

Even if you are buying lumber such as redwood and pine, finished smooth and parallel on all four surfaces, there can still be damaged edges. There may be stones and staples embedded and the edges may be dented. Forklifts can mangle edges, causing board

When gluing up boards to make a sign panel, number them in sequence. Use a straight edge to line up where they will be joined with dowels or biscuits.

edges to crack and splinter. A board can also have a crook that needs to be removed. And a wood like redwood usually has a rounded edge. You may also discover, after buying your board, that there is a crack in it. Take note that crack-free boards are essential to sign carving. Since most cracks run parallel to the grain, the solution might be to saw out the crack and rejoin the pieces.

The table saw is the tool of choice when ripping, though a hand circular saw and a straight edge can also do the job. More and more home centers and lumber companies offer the service of ripping boards to size and some will even join them for a fee. A jointer will also produce a flat edge on a board. But the tool is expensive and is not effective when the edge is very irregular or has a large crook.

JOINING

After you have ripped your lumber and gotten the edges as straight and parallel as possible, check over the wood, look for any other imperfections, and lay out your wood good side up. If you are using pine, and knots are visible, they must be tight and not in an area that will be carved. If a knot is loose, it will have to be drilled out and plugged with a round piece of the same wood.

If you have several boards to join up, arrange and rearrange them until the edges are as flush as possible. With a softwood like redwood, there will be some give so clamping will close up the space if there is a slight gap between the boards. When a slight gap is unavoidable, make sure that the space is in the middle of the span, not at the ends. If there are gaps at the ends, it would be advisable to rerip the boards.

Before you are ready to join the boards, number or letter them: 1–1, 2–2 or A–A, B–B. Doing this means that the time spent arranging the boards for the best fit won't be wasted with guesswork when it comes time to glue them up.

DOWELS AND BISCUITS

Traditionally woodworkers have joined boards using dowels inserted between them. The dowels, however, do not necessarily make for a better bond. The straight edges of the boards do that. The purpose of the dowels when edge-gluing boards is to keep the tops of the boards relatively flush when they are clamped together. The dowels also prevent the boards from sliding apart while the glue is still wet.

If you are using a doweling jig, available at almost all home centers and hardware stores, a ³/₈" thick dowel will work for joining most boards. A ¹/₄" dowel is too thin and will easily break when the boards are forced together; and a ¹/₂" dowel will be too close to the surface, especially if using thin boards.

Doweling is not difficult. It means putting marks on adjacent boards so that when holes are drilled perpendicular to the board's edge, a dowel will mate in those holes. To locate where the holes will be, you can use a T-square. Essentially a ruler with a crossbar at one end, this tool can span a number of boards and will allow you to mark where your dowels will go.

When doweling the edges of boards, you will need to go dead center on each edge to keep the board surfaces flush and prevent the dowels from being too close to one of the surfaces. Some doweling jigs are self-centering, while others are gauged so that the adjustment depends on the width of the board. If a board is 1" thick, the jig has a setting for ¹/₂".

In addition to the doweling jig, you will need an electric drill and drill bit. You will have to mark the drill bit or use a depth gauge to determine the depth of the hole. It should be only slightly deeper than half the length of the dowel. A good length for a dowel, especially for large signs, is 3". This puts 1¹/₂" of dowel into each board being joined.

What is fast replacing the doweling jig is the plate or biscuit joiner. Instead of drilling dowel holes, these hand-held machines cut slots in the boards that are to be joined. Wooden biscuits go into these slots. The biscuit, made of compressed wood, swells when set in glue.

There are several advantages to using the biscuit joiner. The machine cuts the slots—using a small rotary carbide cutter—very quickly. It also makes an oversized lengthwise slot, which is more forgiving than a dowel hole and allows for some play when joining boards edge to edge. The slot cutter makes for a uniform depth, so depth gauges are unnecessary. And the biscuit makes for a very strong joint.

A doweling jig is an inexpensive tool to facilitate joining boards. By drilling into the edges of the boards to be joined, you make holes for dowels that will keep the boards flush when the glue is drying.

A tool more expensive than the doweling jig for joining boards is the biscuit joiner. The tool creates slots into which biscuit-shaped pieces of wood are inserted. These not only keep the boards flush but also help create a strong bond.

1. The best glue for joining up signs that will be displayed outdoors is WEST System®, a two-part epoxy. A pump dispenses the resin. The smaller can contains a hardener that will be added to the resin in a 4:1 mix.

2. Use pipe or bar clamps to glue up a sign panel. Pictured is an oval sign panel being joined.

3. Clamps should be alternated top and bottom to keep the panel (or sign) flat.

4. Use additional clamps such as C or cam clamps to hold the pipe clamps tight against the boards.

Despite these advantages, this is not a machine for the casual user. Even the cheapest models come with a hefty price tag. But for a woodworking enthusiast doing a variety of projects that need joining, it is a must-have piece of equipment.

WEST System®

If you are gluing up a signboard and it is going to be displayed outdoors, you must use waterproof glue.

Some new glues on the market claim to be waterproof, though with limitations. Labels may indicate that the bond will not hold if the wood is submersed in water. But some waterproof glues have been around for decades and have proven themselves to hold under the worst conditions. The best product and most useful to the sign carver is WEST System®.

The glue's name is an acronym: Wood Epoxy Saturation System. It was developed as a way to make wood harder and exclude moisture. Today it is most commonly used in the boatbuilding industry. Its properties are remarkable. Not only does it need minimal pressure for bonding, but it is also gap-filling. This means that two pieces do not have to be mated perfectly flush for a strong bond. And it can be applied underwater! The glue will also bond metal to wood, and it can be used to build up damaged or missing surfaces.

Like all epoxies, WEST System® is a two-part product that requires mixing a resin and a hardener. A convenient feature of the system is the two pumps that premeasure each part.

WEST System® offers a slow set and a fast set epoxy. The slow set takes 9 to 12 hours to harden, the fast set 4 to 6 hours. Working time is often critical when gluing up boards because it takes so long to apply the glue; it is best to work with the slow set epoxy. This has a working time of about 45 minutes before it starts to get tacky.

Another successful waterproof glue is Resorcinol. This comes in the form of a liquid resin and a powder catalyst. Resorcinol does not come with pumps; it requires the use of measuring tools to determine the correct amounts.

Epoxies are best applied to the surfaces to be mated using utility brushes. These are available at hardware stores at nominal cost and are disposable. When spreading the glue on the wood, make sure you have covered the surfaces completely. A thick coating is not necessary because much of the glue will be squeezed out when the wood is clamped together.

CLAMPING

When edge gluing boards to produce a panel of wood, pipe or bar clamps are essential. Set up your clamps across saw horses with some covering on the floor or ground under the work area. Glue squeeze-out is inevitable, and the glue will drip and leave a mess that is difficult to remove.

Pipe clamps work best when they are alternated top and bottom on the sign panel. If you have one clamp on the bottom, you place the next clamp in line on the top of the panel. Continue alternating along the length of the panel. Clamping on only one side puts too much pressure across the panel, causing the wood to form a cupped or bowed shape. And excessive pressure could cause the boards to pop apart.

How far apart should your pipe clamps be spaced? A good rule of thumb to follow is to have at least one clamp every foot with a clamp very near each end of the panel. If you are gluing up an 8' sign panel, then you would use nine clamps: five on the bottom and four on the top.

A great deal of pressure does not have to be exerted when tightening the clamps, but you do want to look for a uniform glue squeeze-out along the seams. It is also a good idea to use C or cam clamps to hold the pipe or bar clamps to the panel. Putting clamps on clamps will insure that the panel stays flat.

A word of caution when clamping with WEST System®: the epoxy can form a strong bond between the wood and the metal of the clamp. You must be careful, then, when removing the clamp from the sign to avoid pulling away a chunk of wood along with the metal. If a clamp has bonded to the wood, hit the clamp lightly with a hammer at the bond.

Also be warned that epoxy glues defy removal from clothing. When gluing, make sure you wear disposable coveralls or clothes that are relegated to the workshop.

SANDING

There are many different sanding devices available on the market: orbital, pneumatic, flap, belt, stroke and drum sanders. Sanders such as the random orbital ones are not meant for a lot of wood removal but are well suited for finish sanding. The belt sander works best for sanding signs.

A belt sander is a surfacing machine that uses a continuous abrasive belt. Typical belt sanders have sanding belts that measure 3" x 21" and 4" x 24". The bigger the machine, the faster it finishes the sanding, but it is going to weigh more.

For sanding the sign flat, which means removing the glue squeeze-out and peaks and valleys created by the joined boards, you need only two belts: 50 and 80 grit. Any grit coarser than this will leave too many deep scratches. Any grit finer is unnecessary. It should be pointed out here that although you want your sign to look smooth and finished, you are not working on a piece of furniture. In most cases you will be painting your sign, and even if you stain it, an 80-grit belt will leave an appropriately smooth surface.

Sanding a sign is really a two-stage operation. With the coarser 50-grit, you will be removing ridges and glue buildup. The 80-grit belt will do the final smoothing.

SANDING TIPS

First, make sure your work surface is free of foreign objects and is as evenly flat and as smooth as possible. Any raised areas on the work surface will be telegraphed into the sign panel. Sand the back of the sign first. You can get away with just the 50-grit belt for the back, especially if it is to be mounted to a wall.

If you are working on a long sign panel, one 4' or longer, it is best to sand it in sections. This means doing an area only two or three feet long while standing in one place. Sanding too large an area may have you tripping over a cord or losing your concentration. In fact, you will not get an evenly sanded surface if you parade up and down a sign.

Another sanding tip is to keep the sander from angling across the grain, which will cause scratches. Also keep the sander moving without exerting unnecessary pressure. Leaving it in one spot will cause it to dig in and produce an uneven surface; pressing down on the sander will also cause an irregular surface.

Clamping the sign down is also important, but make sure you place the clamp where it will not interfere with the sanding. A very large sign will probably stay in place owing to its weight, but it is wise to have a stop block at the one end of the work surface; this is in the event the sander forces the sign to travel with the revolving belt.

New sanding belts are a joy to work with. Do not hesitate to replace old ones for the job. But even these can get clogged quickly, so have on hand a rubber belt cleaner and use it frequently. The more you use it, the less likely the belt will fill up with dust.

When a belt does get dull, you don't have to throw it away.

Though many sanding devices are available, the belt sander is the best for signs. The one pictured has a belt that measures 4" wide by 24" long.

Keep the belt from getting clogged with dust and grit. Use a rubber belt cleaner.

After belt sanding, you can do finish-sanding with a cushioned palm sander. It is also a good sanding device to clean up slight imperfections left by the belt sander.

Because of its size and maneuverability, the saber saw is an excellent choice for cutting away the edges of glued-up sign panels.

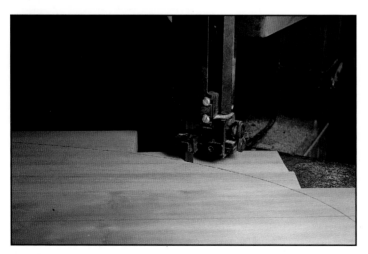

An alternative to the saber saw is the bandsaw. But a large sign is difficult to push through the blade of the tool.

Cut it up and use the pieces to make sanding pads. There are always areas to touch up on the sign.

Sanding frames are available to prevent the sander from tilting and gouging the work. The frame clips to the bottom of the sander and acts like a baseplate.

Dust bags come with most models and are indispensible when sanding indoors. The alternative is to sand your sign outside.

LOOKING FOR IMPERFECTIONS

The final sanding tip is the "five o'clock shadow test." Take a utility light or a portable light source, not a fluorescent, and hold it at a severe angle to the sign. You will be amazed at the number of sanding imperfections revealed. Walk along the length of the sign and circle any imperfections you find with a pencil. Large imperfections will have to be belt sanded. Small ones can be handled with a sanding pad. Use a block of wood and a piece of worn sanding belt. Cushioned hand sanding pads with stick-on sanding discs are easier to use. Sanding supplies are available from most woodworking catalogs (see Buyer's Guide).

REPAIRS

Now is the time to go over the sign panel once again and check for chips, cracks or other imperfections. Signs to be painted are the easiest to deal with because fillers can be used and covered over with paint. Exterior fillers are available for the job. If a splinter of wood comes off an edge, use the WEST System® to replace the piece of wood since little pressure is required with this epoxy. For a dent, you can apply a wet rag to the area and the grain will eventually "pop out," bringing the dented area flush to the surface. Dowels are sometimes used as plugs for repair, but they are not recommended because their end grain will show through paint.

Cutting to Size

Many tools and machines are available for cutting and trimming your sign to finished size. A radial arm saw or a table saw will trim irregular ends, and a bandsaw will will take care of curves. But a cost-effective and useful tool that can accomplish these jobs is the saber saw. This portable saw, with its variety of blades and power, can go where other machines dare not go; it can plunge into the interior of a panel to cut away wood. A variety of blades is available, but be aware that blades with more teeth per inch cut smoother than blades with fewer teeth. Although a bandsaw might seem a better choice than the saber saw for cutting out profiles, large signs are difficult to maneuver against the rotating blade. The saber saw cuts curved profiles easily. It can also cut out an interior area of the sign panel without an entrance cut from the outside perimeter.

A tool for squaring up the sign, meaning that you want to cut the ends perpendicular to the sides, is the portable circular saw. This powerhouse tool can be held with one hand and has an adjustable base that allows you to regulate the depth of cut. After using the circular saw, you should go over the cut edges with a belt sander. An 80-grit belt will do fine for the edges, even the narrowest belt will be wider than your thickest sign, and the sander will also handle convex or outside curves.

There are two ways to deal with concave or inside curves made by the saber saw or the bandsaw. You can use a drum sander in an electric drill. The pair of tools will smooth out these curves, but it will take a steady hand to prevent chattermarks and unwanted bevels. Alternately you can use sandpaper wrapped around a wood dowel.

The Routed Edge

Nearly every woodworker has a router. It is considered the most versatile of all shop tools because it shapes and cuts. It will cut grooves, make decorative edges, even make wood joints. It is five times faster than the fastest drill and the heaviest router weighs less than 10 pounds.

For those who are not familiar with the router, it consists basically of an enclosed motor with two handles, one on each side.

Use a sanding drum in a power drill to smooth concave profiles.

A router bit or cutter is secured in a chuck located on the lower end of the motor, which is tightened with a wrench. The depth of the cut is regulated by moving the motor up and down and locking it in place.

The four bits most frequently used by sign carvers are the cove, the bevel, the beading and the v-grooving bit. The cove bit makes for a concave edge that sign carvers often accentuate with gold leaf. Cove bits are available in sizes from $1/8$" radius to 1". The bevel bit leaves a slanting edge with a 45-degree angle. The beading bit produces an edge that is rounded over and sometimes stepped down slightly to produce a shadow line.

What makes for a very classy border, however, is a v-groove just inside the edge of the sign. To create this cut you will need a

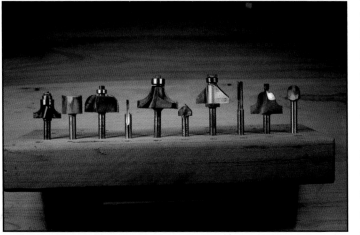

Router bits are the tools of choice when putting fancy edges on a sign.

router edge guide and some practice so that your bit does not stray to the edge of the board. If you can perfect the technique of routing the v-groove, which is especially difficult on curves, your sign will have a unique look, and the groove can be painted a contrasting color or gold leafed.

Router bits come in two varieties: high speed steel and carbide-tipped. The bits made with high speed steel, while cheaper, do not stay sharp as long as their carbide counterparts and may burn the wood. But carbide bits are universally available and have literally pushed the other bits out of the market.

Use a router and guide to put a decorative v-shaped cut inside the edge of a sign.

CHAPTER THREE

DESIGN AND LAYOUT

Choosing the shape, design and location of a sign offers almost limitless possibilities. Though the most common sign is rectangular with square corners, signs can be cut with radius corners, they can be oval, triangular, ribbon-shaped, or whatever the imagination comes up with. Signs can also have appliques, which are added pieces of wood, carved and glued to the surface. And they can be mounted against buildings, suspended from brackets or hung on posts.

Though simple house number and name signs don't require much design consideration other than color, shape and letter style, you may want to try your hand at something more challenging, perhaps a sign that includes a logo of your business. For some ideas, see some examples in the book's gallery of finished signs.

Whatever design you settle on, a key factor will be the letter style. What has made signwork so much easier for the professional sign carver are stick-on or transfer letters. Hundreds of styles and sizes are available and nearly all art supply stores carry them. Two common brands are Zipatone® and Letraset™. Some lettering styles frequently used in the sign trade are Roman, block and script. (See the type section in the back of this book.) Foreign

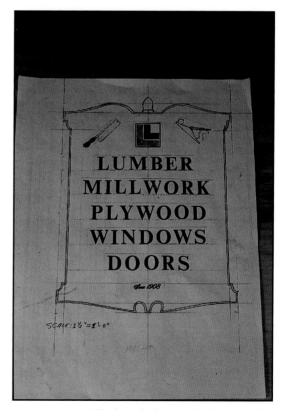

Black and white scale drawing of sign proposal using transfer letters.

Another scale drawing with transfer letters. The drawing includes customer-supplied artwork.

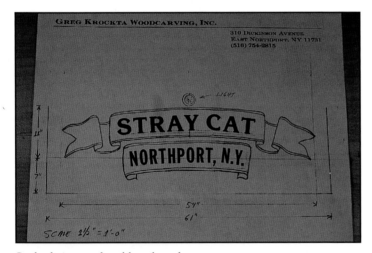

Scale drawing of a ribbon board boat sign.

lettering and antique styles are available. Books of alphabets can also be purchased. Books not only offer letter styles but also help with spacing. Be aware that letters come in point sizes. A 144 point capital letter, an "A" for example, will measure about 1$\frac{5}{8}$" tall.

ENLARGING

With transfer letters, you can get started with just a piece of paper and parallel lines. Using small letters on a standard size piece of paper, you can mock up a sign design. This design can then be enlarged using a copying machine or an opaque projector. The projector is designed to project an image of a non-transparent object onto a screen or wall. Opaque projectors range considerably in sizes and prices. But having one allows you to enlarge a pattern while your sketch is projected onto a wall. If you are carving professionally, you may need to take a logo from a business card, a newspaper, menu or piece of stationery and incorporate it into your sign. The opaque projector allows you to do that. The projector also makes it possible to enlarge existing letters from alphabet books or transfer sheets for a sign.

When using the projector, one which is able to accept a magazine, book, photograph or any sheet of paper, you need to have a flat surface to place it on and a flat wall to project the image on. The best pattern paper to use is craft paper because it is strong and will not tear easily. If you are looking to enlarge letters, draw parallel lines on the paper, spacing them to represent the height you want for the letters. Next, securely tape the craft paper to the wall. You don't want the paper's weight pulling it down or your own hand pressure ripping it away from the wall.

Once you have projected the letters onto the paper between your parallel lines, you can start drawing. If you are using a block style with lots of straight sides, a wooden or steel ruler will be a big aid. Curves will have to be done freehand.

After tracing the letters, turn on the lights and check to see that you haven't missed any lines. The letters need to look right before you transfer them to the wood. Professional sign carvers especially need to check that names, addresses and phone numbers

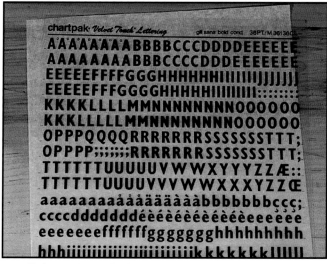

1. Full sheet of transfer letters.

2. Use an opaque projector to project a scale drawing on a wall for enlarging.

3. Drawing letters projected on the wall by the opaque projector.

4. Once the full-size pattern is established, copy it onto the signboard using carbon paper.

5. A T-square is useful for drawing the straight edges of letters.

21

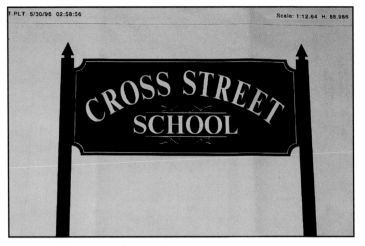

A computer-generated scale drawing.

A computer-generated template allows you to carve letters in the cutout areas.

are correct. It is no big deal to change a number on paper. It is a big deal in wood.

CARBON PAPER

Carbon paper is the simplest of tools and one of the most frequently used by sign carvers. Most of us are familiar with the blue-black carbon paper that leaves our fingertips looking as if they have been to the police station. But carbon paper takes other forms. One of them is white carbon, particularly useful when transferring patterns onto a dark surface. Another is graphite paper, which leaves what looks like a pencil line that is erasable. There is also available a heavy duty carbon paper that will leave a very dark impression.

When using carbon paper to transfer your paper pattern design to the signboard, you want to tape the paper pattern to the board so that it does not move. Then you can slip the carbon paper between the pattern and the wood, making sure that you do not move the pattern. A ballpoint pen works better than a pencil for the tracing. You can press harder with a pen. A pencil dulls and may even break. T-squares and rulers are also helpful when drawing over straight lines.

For very large signs with massive logos and letters where using carbon is impractical, you can use a pounce wheel. With its ratchet-like teeth, the pounce wheel will perforate the pattern outlines with a series of holes. You can then take this perforated paper to the sign and spread chalk line powder over the paper, leaving a colored outline on the wood. From there you can outline with pen.

COMPUTERS

Computer generated lettering will most probably replace transfer letters and opaque projectors. Today computers not only generate a vast array of lettering styles and logos, but they can also generate a vinyl template. As a professional sign carver, you can paint your sign, lay the vinyl template over it, then carve and gold leaf the letters before removing it. The template provides a perfect mask for the areas around the letters and makes for less gold leaf cleanup later on.

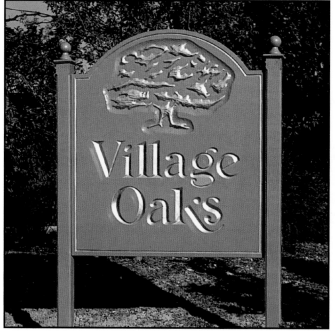

The background of this sign has been removed to make the tree stand out in relief. Note the nice shapes of the lowercase letters used for the words.

The sign for a private community shows several sign carving techniques. The script lettering has been gold leafed, the egret was carved and appliqued, and the cattails in the background were v-carved.

Appliques add color and dimension to signs. Here, appliqued pumpkins give a spark of interest to a simple sign.

Aluminum leaf can be used in two ways, as this sign demonstrates. The letters are bright and shiny, while the nickel has been "antiqued." Antiquing is achieved by brushing thinned-down paint over the aluminum leaf and then wiping it off until a desired effect is reached.

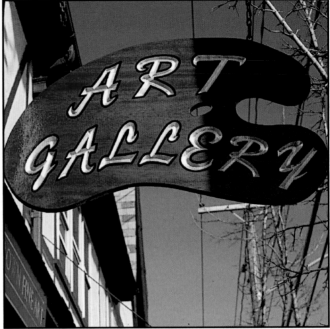

Two Canadian geese make a beautiful applique on this simple oval sign with a double gold leaf border. A plain metal bracket completes the look.

Some signs are of a recognizable shape. This art gallery chose an artist's palette.

The logo on top makes an otherwise boring sign very attractive. The letters were carved and painted white.

Teal and aqua have become popular colors. The oyster shell, with all its layers, is a very nice shape to carve. It fits in well with a nautical theme, especially on this sign, which was made for a town by the seashore.

A teak ribbon board makes a real classic-looking boat sign. The ribbon board is actually two pieces of teak bent and surface glued together to follow the curve of the boat's transom.

This sign is near Roslyn Harbor, New York, the home of well-known folk artist Tom Langan. He carved the great blue heron that appears on this sign.

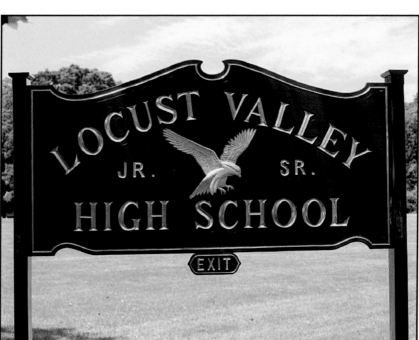

Here's a perfect way to handle a sign for co-ops. The large top sign is permanent, but the two smaller information signs underneath will be removed after all the co-ops are sold.

Dark green, sometimes referred to as hunter or forest green, is by far the most popular background color for signs. The falcon applique is a difficult piece to carve with lots of realistic detail carving.

Real rope adds an interesting touch to the border of this sign. Also note the Old English lettering style and the brightly painted sunset.

The lettering on this sign was hand drawn to give a special impression. The plaques of the owners were added to the sign after it was carved.

The shape of this sign, the lettering and the banner all combine to give it a "Roaring Twenties" look. The banner was relief-carved as well as appliqued.

This unusually shaped sign features fancy lettering and a lamppost that was entirely appliqued.

The type style used for this sign is called Arnold Bocklin. A colorful sunburst adds a touch of color to a brown background.

Two colors are often more attractive on a sign than one color. The top piece of this sign adds a second color and a decorative touch.

Not using gold leaf can be just as dramatic depending on a sign's function. This vertical sign features carved and painted letters and decor.

This ten-foot-long ribbon board was made from three pieces of mahogany. The ends were added on from behind. The lettering at the bottom of the sign is gold on a flat surface. Notice how it doesn't appear as shiny as the carved letters.

A close-up shows the detail in a very elaborate appliqued carving of flowers. The sign's background is unstained, varnished mahogany.

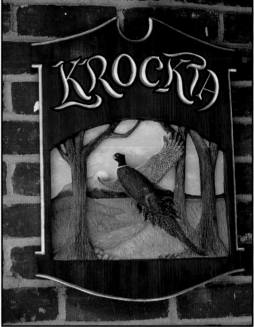

The author's own house sign. The pheasant scene was relief carved in two-inch-thick pine and appliqued, giving it an extremely three-dimensional look.

This sign is composed of three layers. The oval is the first layer; the banner and flowers form the second layer; and a few flowers on top of the banner make the third.

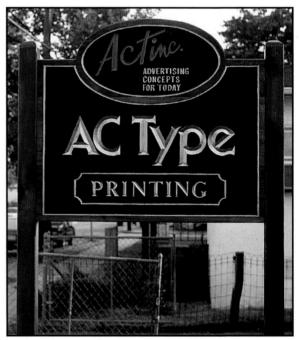

You can't beat the visibility of gold leaf on a black background. The varnished cedar posts add a nice "woody" feel to the sign.

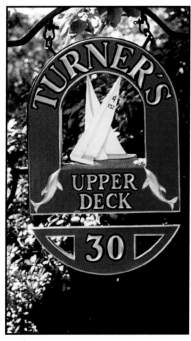

Appliques, such as the gold-leafed wave on this stained and varnished mahogany sign, add interest and visibility to signs. The thin v-grooves on the logo were painted black.

A lot of work went into this very ornate house sign. The wood around the sailboats was cut out, the dolphins were appliqued, and a separate hanging number sign was created. A custom-made wrought iron bracket gives the finishing touches.

The appliqued mahogany ship's wheel gives this sign a real nautical look. Stars can sometimes add a nice touch to a sign.

Here, a plain sign is dressed up with a leaf design.

Without the pineapple, this would be a typical estate sign: simple shape, black background, gold leafed letters and edge, and metal post or stake. A pineapple is a nice-looking decoration and a symbol of hospitality.

This sign, carved for a housing development, has a very "corporate" look. Note the tree reflection: gold leaf on a flat surface.

A rare find these days, this sign has no gold leafing. The word "Tara" has been gouge carved.

Aluminum leaf was the obvious choice for this sign due to the word "Silver" in the name.

A typical ribbon board boat sign is made unusual by the use of a gray background and aluminum leaf.

Some boat owners like quarterboards, name signs that appear on both sides of the boat. These two were carved with a simple fan design on the ends.

Below: Weather can be hard on signs. This photo was taken several years after the sign was first installed and just after it was repainted.

Above: This contemporary-looking sign, mounted on a nice stone wall with flowers on top, marks a residential community. It was recently repainted.

31

Here's a real eye-catcher. The skates, hockey stick, puck, baseballs and helmet were all handcarved. The baseball bat is a real bat sawed in half.

Occasionally, customers prefer the letters finished in a color. The top two signs were carved and painted white, while the bottom signs were computer generated white vinyl. The signs on this directory are removable to accommodate new tenants.

What better sign for a lumber yard than stained and varnished Honduras mahogany. The appliqued hammer and chisel were hand carved. The finial on top is a hand carved pineapple.

Three inch wide steel straps on both sides keep this two-sided 4' by 7' hanging sign from warping. A very large wood post is needed for a sign this size.

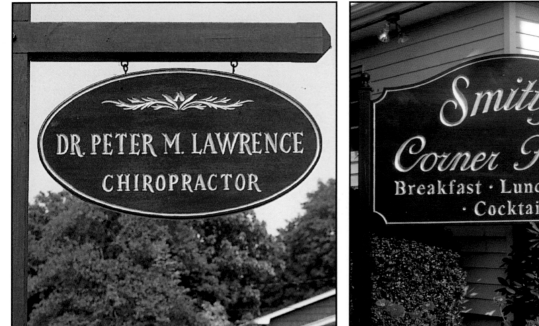

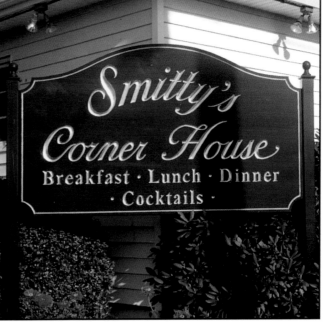

When an office is in an area that's zoned residential, most towns will only permit a small sign like this one.

Script lettering gives this restaurant sign a fancier, more elegant look. The green background and posts were chosen so that the sign would blend in with its surroundings.

Some people have special brick or stone walls built for the sign to be mounted either on top of the wall or on the wall's face. Two pieces of molding give this sign a more colonial look.

This contemporary layout is a logo just as it is. The look is very common nowadays due to the widespread use of computers in design.

A bright red sign certainly gets attention. Posts that are painted in a contrasting color can add to the attention-getting power of the sign; posts the same color can sometimes get lost when viewed from a distance.

Most oval free-standing signs require a metal band around the entire edge of the sign to prevent warping.

Almost anything can be carved on a sign, even an antique car. The metal straps help keep the sign from warping and also give it a more rustic look, especially against the weathered wall.

These street signs, complete with posts and metal brackets, were designed in conjunction with the houses in this private community.

A lot of thought and effort went into the presentation of this sign. The roof not only looks nice but will help protect the sign from the weather. Landscaping around a sign can add a lot of interest.

Sign carving and nautical themes go hand in hand. On this sign, the clipper ship was appliqued and the gilded rope edge was hand carved.

For a change, the background is carved and gilded to create a very graphic corporate logo. A little green suggests leaves.

This very large sign measures 4½ feet tall and 32 feet long. The installation required a crane, bucket truck, welder and four people.

The windmill is a relief carved plaque applied separately to this large mahogany sign. The lettering across the bottom was carved and painted white. The posts are cedar.

Most wood signs have a medium to dark background. However, some customers are willing to sacrifice some visibility in order to match or complement their building. In this case, a dark outline around the gold letters is almost essential.

Horizontal Shapes

Most signs are a horizontal shape. Some suggestions for: corners - 1-4, 7, 9; ends - 5, 6, 8, 10-12; tops - 13-21, 26-28; tops and bottoms - 22-25, 29, 30.

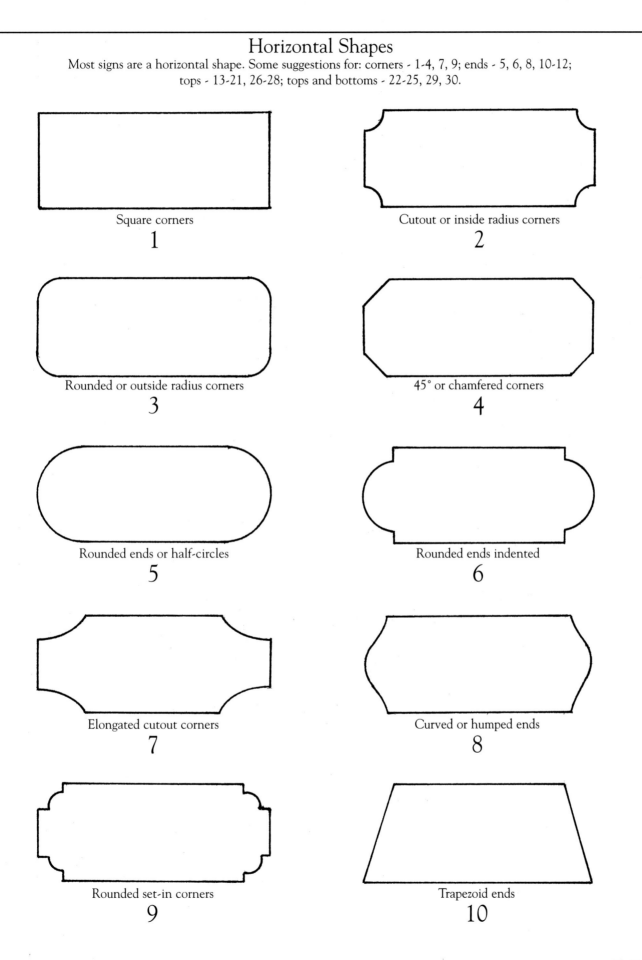

Square corners
1

Cutout or inside radius corners
2

Rounded or outside radius corners
3

45° or chamfered corners
4

Rounded ends or half-circles
5

Rounded ends indented
6

Elongated cutout corners
7

Curved or humped ends
8

Rounded set-in corners
9

Trapezoid ends
10

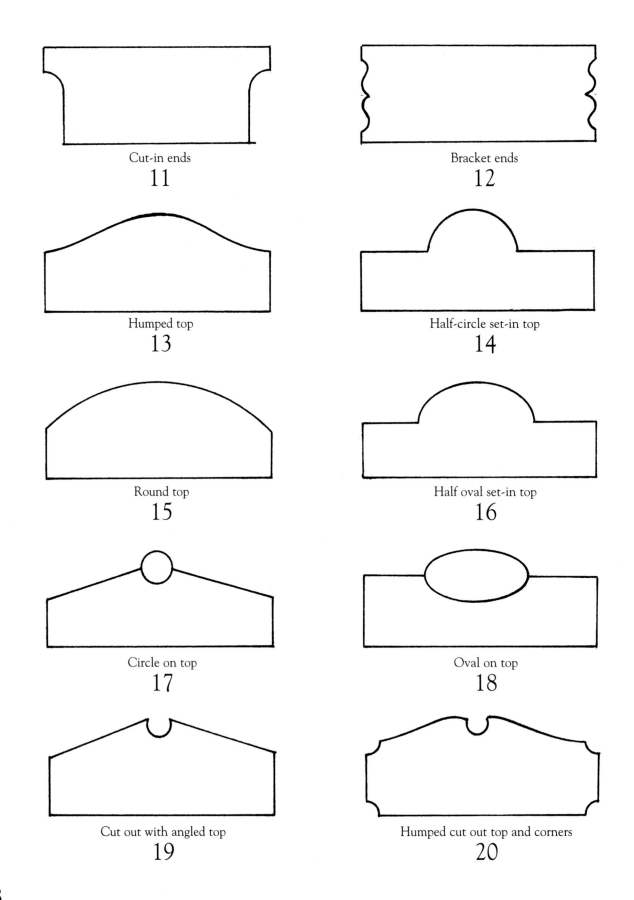

Cut-in ends
11

Bracket ends
12

Humped top
13

Half-circle set-in top
14

Round top
15

Half oval set-in top
16

Circle on top
17

Oval on top
18

Cut out with angled top
19

Humped cut out top and corners
20

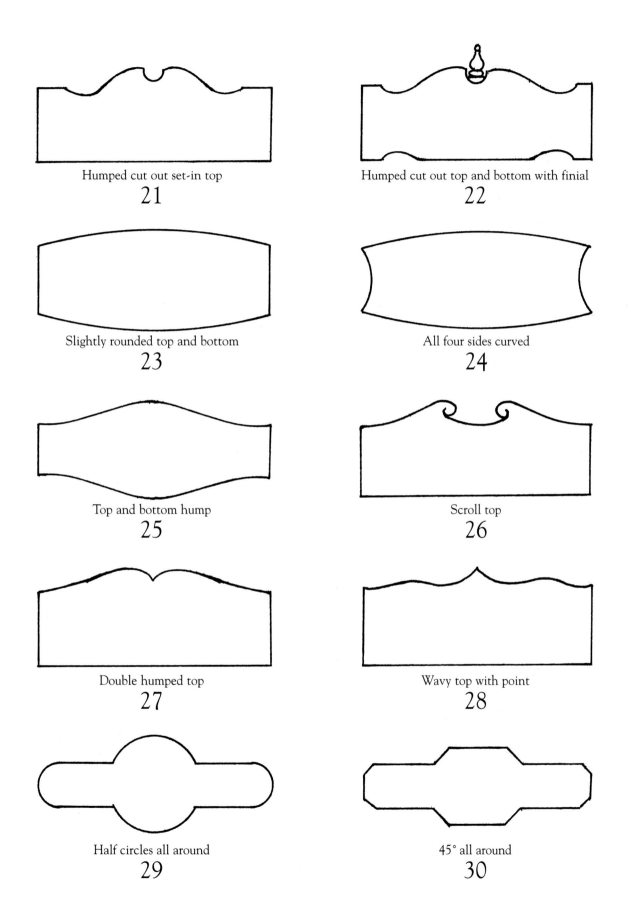

Humped cut out set-in top
21

Humped cut out top and bottom with finial
22

Slightly rounded top and bottom
23

All four sides curved
24

Top and bottom hump
25

Scroll top
26

Double humped top
27

Wavy top with point
28

Half circles all around
29

45° all around
30

Vertical Shapes
Some signs are a vertical shape, commonly used for house signs and plaques

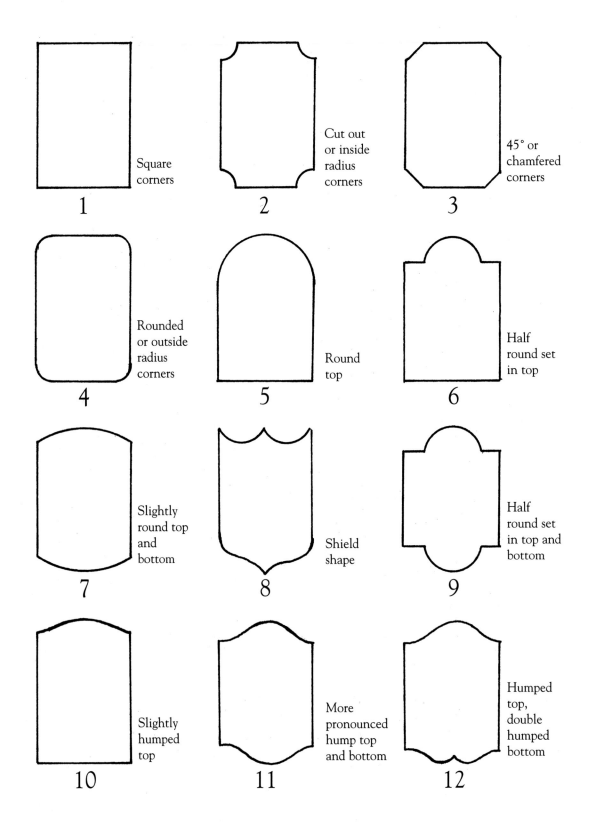

Square
corners

1

Cut out
or inside
radius
corners

2

45° or
chamfered
corners

3

Rounded
or outside
radius
corners

4

Round
top

5

Half
round set
in top

6

Slightly
round top
and
bottom

7

Shield
shape

8

Half
round set
in top and
bottom

9

Slightly
humped
top

10

More
pronounced
hump top
and bottom

11

Humped
top,
double
humped
bottom

12

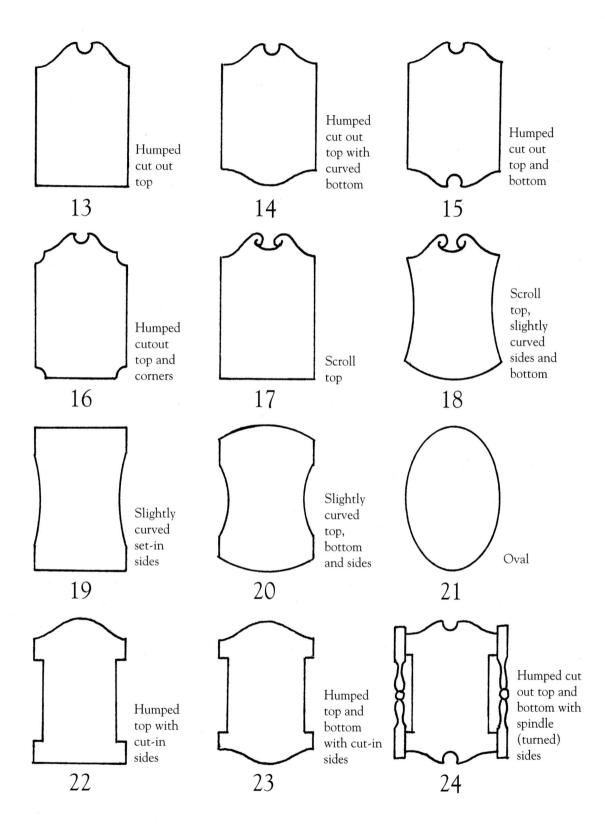

13   Humped cut out top

14   Humped cut out top with curved bottom

15   Humped cut out top and bottom

16   Humped cutout top and corners

17   Scroll top

18   Scroll top, slightly curved sides and bottom

19   Slightly curved set-in sides

20   Slightly curved top, bottom and sides

21   Oval

22   Humped top with cut-in sides

23   Humped top and bottom with cut-in sides

24   Humped cut out top and bottom with spindle (turned) sides

Geometric Shapes
Signs may also be made using a simple geometric shape.

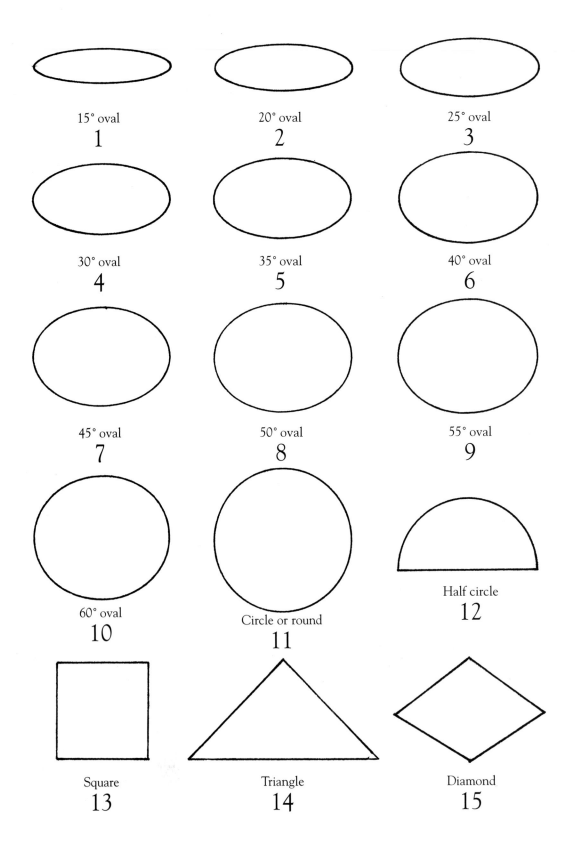

15° oval
1

20° oval
2

25° oval
3

30° oval
4

35° oval
5

40° oval
6

45° oval
7

50° oval
8

55° oval
9

60° oval
10

Circle or round
11

Half circle
12

Square
13

Triangle
14

Diamond
15

Shapes for Hanging

Some shapes look best when hanging underneath another sign, although they could be used on their own.

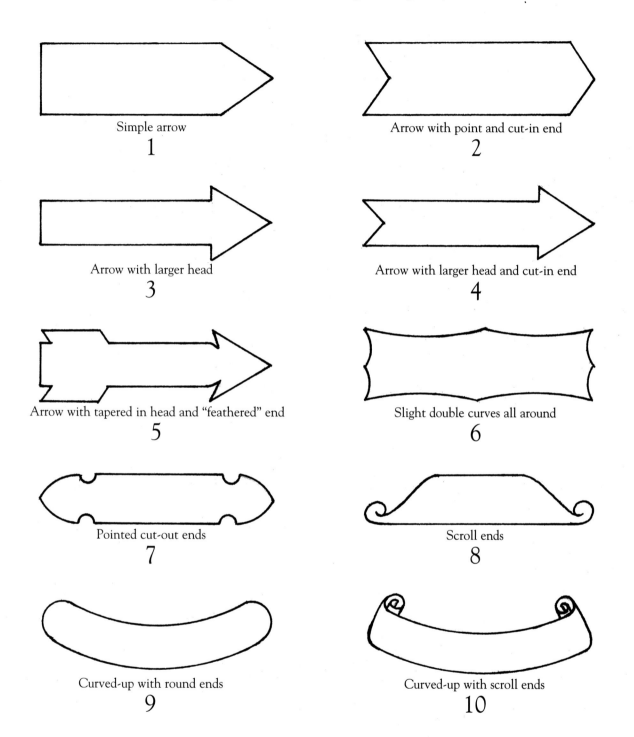

Simple arrow
1

Arrow with point and cut-in end
2

Arrow with larger head
3

Arrow with larger head and cut-in end
4

Arrow with tapered in head and "feathered" end
5

Slight double curves all around
6

Pointed cut-out ends
7

Scroll ends
8

Curved-up with round ends
9

Curved-up with scroll ends
10

Banners and Ribbons

Banners and ribbons are extremely eye-catching when carved in wood.
The 3-dimensional quality is nice to look at and interesting to carve.

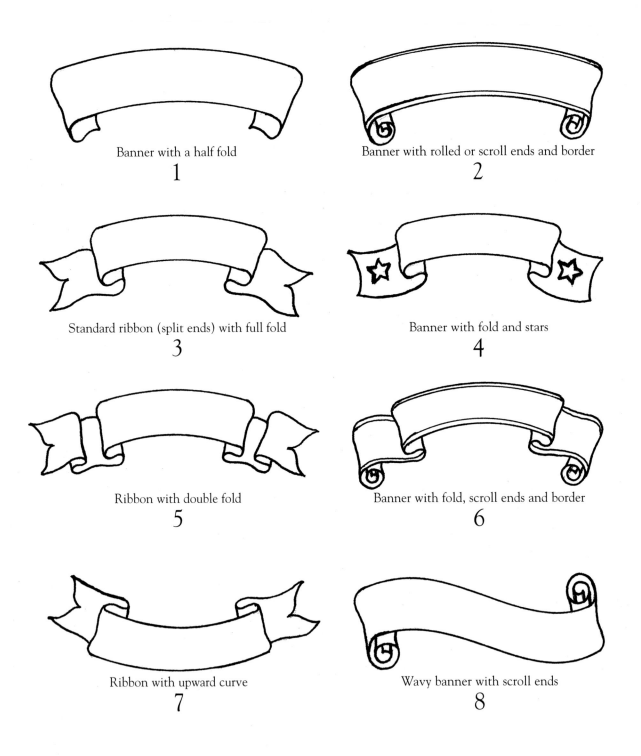

Banner with a half fold
1

Banner with rolled or scroll ends and border
2

Standard ribbon (split ends) with full fold
3

Banner with fold and stars
4

Ribbon with double fold
5

Banner with fold, scroll ends and border
6

Ribbon with upward curve
7

Wavy banner with scroll ends
8

Familiar Shapes

Occassionally a sign is cut to a shape indicating a particular subject or business.

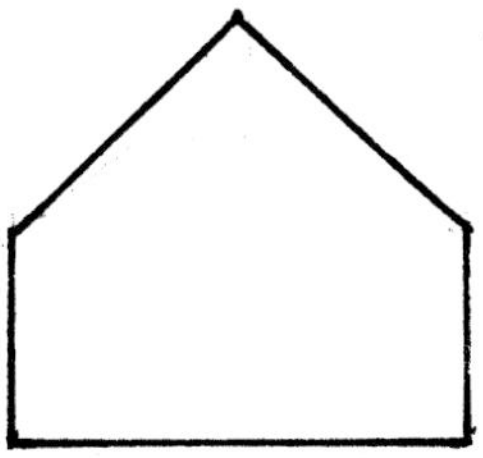

House - Real estate office
1

Star
2

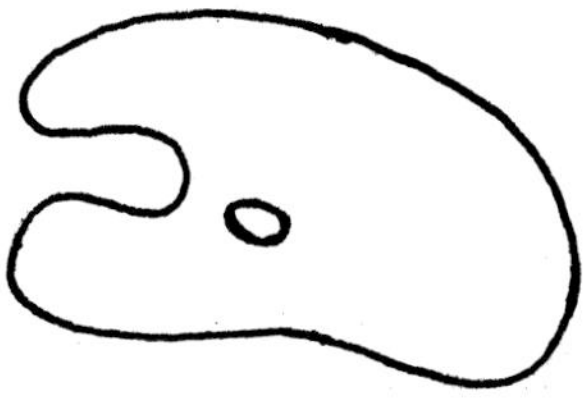

Artist's palette - Art gallery, Art supplies
3

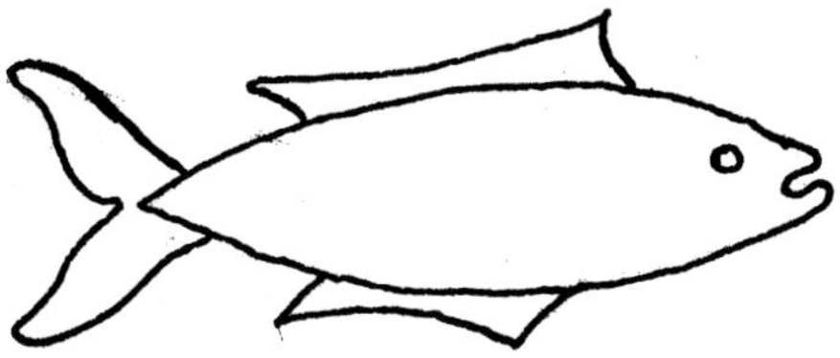

Fish - Seafood store, Bait & tackle
4

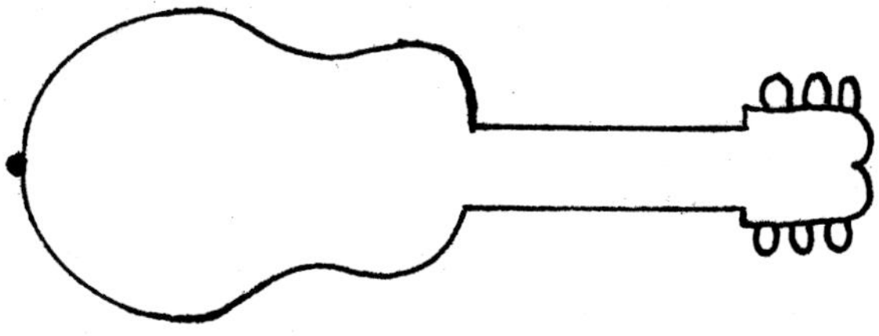

Guitar - Music store, Music teacher
5

Heart - Candy store, Gift shop
6

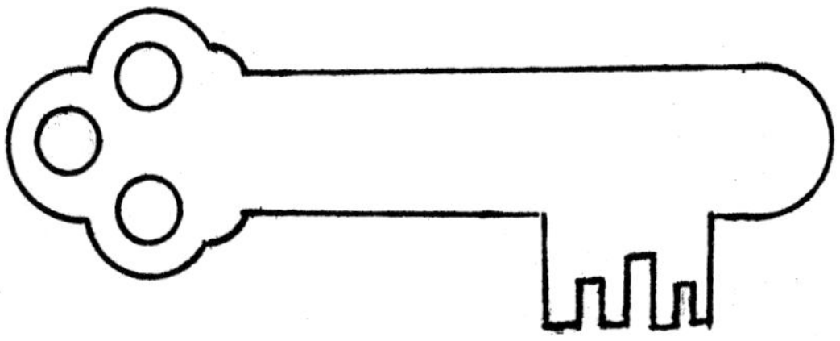

Key - Locksmith
7

Apple - Grocery store, Fruit stand
8

Paddle or oar - Boating supplies
9

Bone - Pet supplies
10

Knife - Restaurant, Butcher
11

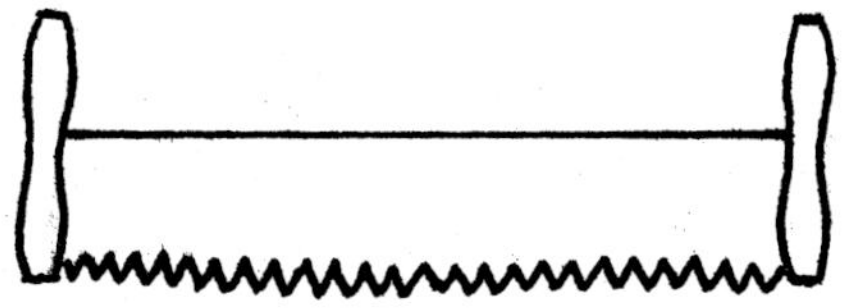

Hand saw - Tree company, Lumber yard, Sawmill
11

45

Borders and Edges
Almost all signs have some kind of border or edge, from plain to ornate.

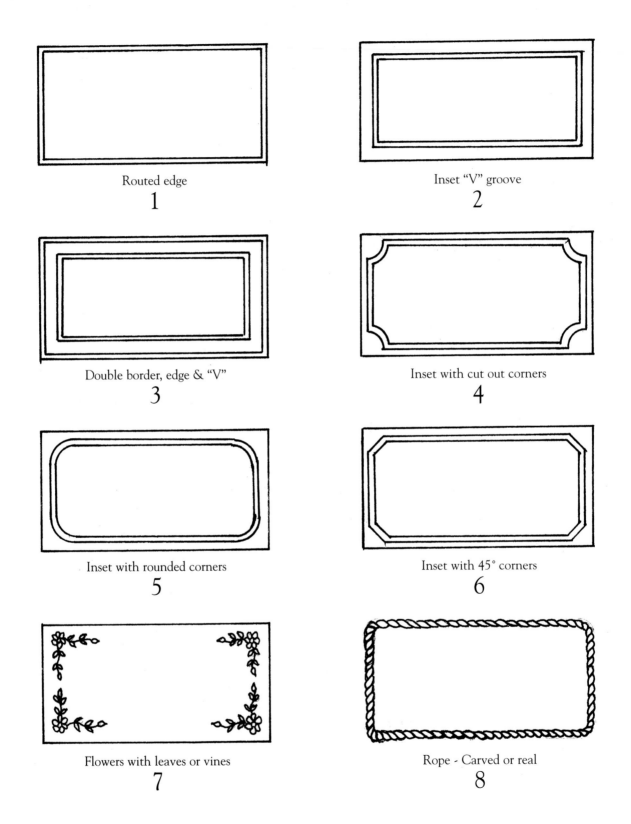

Routed edge
1

Inset "V" groove
2

Double border, edge & "V"
3

Inset with cut out corners
4

Inset with rounded corners
5

Inset with 45° corners
6

Flowers with leaves or vines
7

Rope - Carved or real
8

Posts and Finials

Here are some ideas for posts and finials. All of these can be done in the shop, with the right tools. Many home centers carry various posts as well as tops for numbers 9-13.

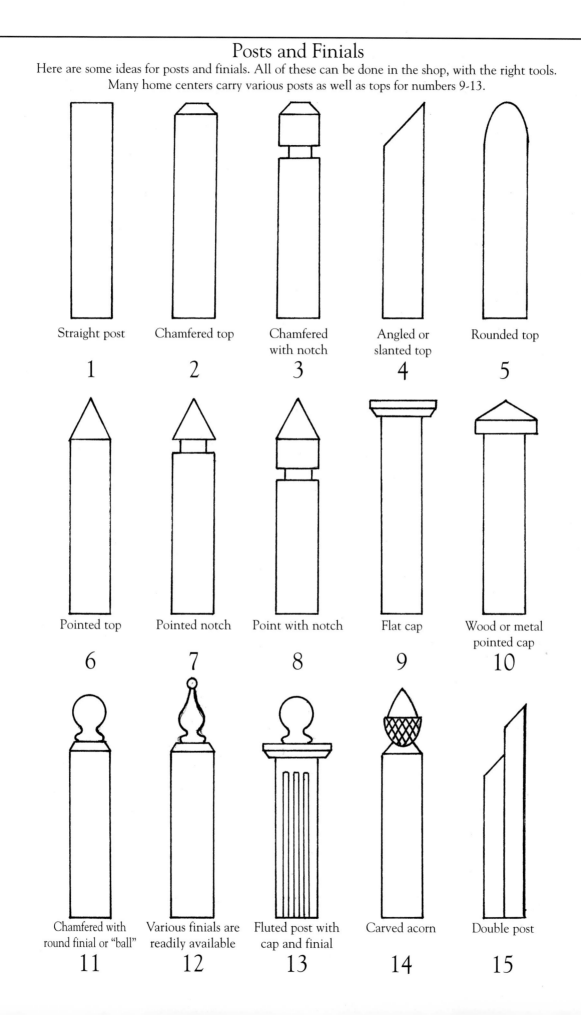

Straight post
1

Chamfered top
2

Chamfered with notch
3

Angled or slanted top
4

Rounded top
5

Pointed top
6

Pointed notch
7

Point with notch
8

Flat cap
9

Wood or metal pointed cap
10

Chamfered with round finial or "ball"
11

Various finials are readily available
12

Fluted post with cap and finial
13

Carved acorn
14

Double post
15

SAMPLE SHAPES

Brackets

Brackets are used for smaller hanging signs. They can be homemade, store bought, or custom made by a blacksmith.

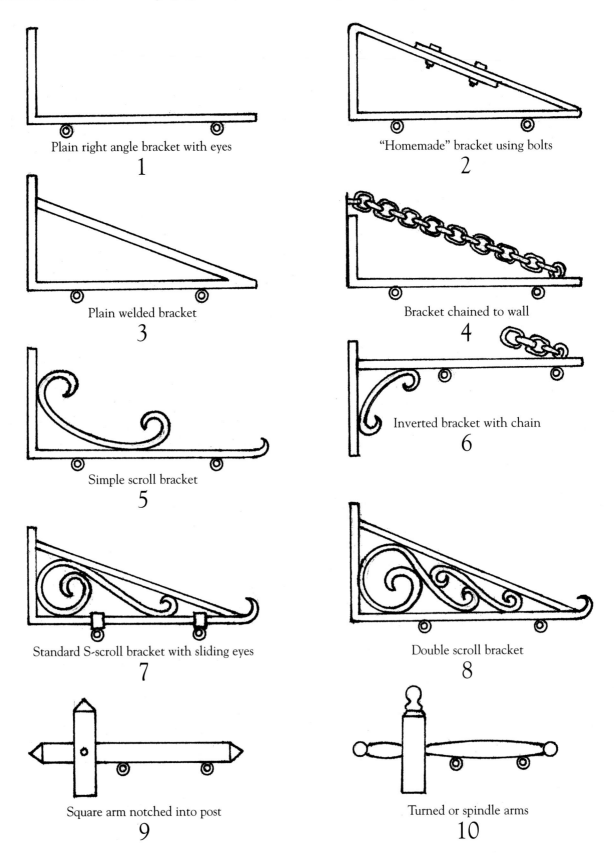

Plain right angle bracket with eyes
1

"Homemade" bracket using bolts
2

Plain welded bracket
3

Bracket chained to wall
4

Simple scroll bracket
5

Inverted bracket with chain
6

Standard S-scroll bracket with sliding eyes
7

Double scroll bracket
8

Square arm notched into post
9

Turned or spindle arms
10

CHAPTER 4

TOOLS AND TECHNIQUES FOR LETTERING

If you look at the cross-section of a carved, incised letter, it will have a v-shape. Even most routed letters have this profile. It is the opposite of relief carving and is actually a form of chip carving. Carving incised letters takes some practice, but their visual appeal is very strong. In fact, it is all that is needed to attract attention and let the viewer know that yours is a handcarved sign.

Some people, however, mistake handcarved signs for routed ones. How can you spot the difference? First, a routed letter will have a uniform depth, unlike the variety of depths achieved with carving different letter styles. The router and its v-grooving bit are limited in that they cannot do some serifs, which are the corners of certain letter styles. And since the width of a letter is limited by the size of the v-grooving bit, the router simply cannot do very wide letters.

For centuries, craftsmen and artisans have relied on a collection of chisels and gouges to make incisions into wood to form letters. A chisel has a flat cutting edge that may be beveled or

The cross-section of two incised or v-shaped letters cut out with a knife. The letter on the left, which is fairly wide, does not have as steep a wall as the narrower letter on the right.

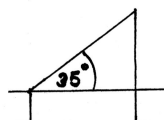

The best tool for carving incised letters is the mill knife. Pictured is an assortment of the knives with blades from 1/2" to 1 1/2" wide (l to r). The four knives on the right were custom made.

tapered on one or both sides while a gouge has a curved cutting edge. The flat, single-beveled chisel held at an angle and tapped with a mallet takes care of the straight cuts. But curved letters need curved tools. So a gouge has to be used to fit a specific curve or at least "walked" around the curve in segmented cuts. On a small, narrow letter, a v-shaped cutting tool is useful for making channels. But the problem with this tool is that it has two cutting edges. While one edge may go with the grain, the other will go against it, thereby crushing the grain and giving a ragged surface. Therefore, a knife with a skewed blade, meaning it has its cutting edge at an angle, is probably best for handling most incised letters.

THE MILL KNIFE

The basic tool for mastering incised letters is the mill knife (see Buyer's Guide). It consists of a high-speed steel blade that slides in and out of a slotted handle and is held in place with a set screw. Typical sizes offer blades that are 1/2", 5/8" and 3/4" wide. The 1/2" size comes with brass fittings and a rosewood handle; the 5/8" and 3/4" sizes with a walnut handle and aluminum fittings.

Since a mill knife comes with an extra long blade, 9" long for the 3/4" size, it needs to be shortened. By holding the edge to a grinding wheel, you not only cut it down to size but you can also create an optimum cutting angle of approximately 35-degrees—the angle measured from an imaginery horizontal line across the width of the blade. Once shortened—by half is fine—you will have a useful knife with an adjustable blade. The adjustment is important because the width of the letters to be carved determines the amount of blade that you want to work with. This means the blade will have to project farther

Because the blade supplied with the mill knife is longer than need-ed, it is necessary to grind it in half. Grinding should be done to approximate the angle you will need at the cutting end of the blade.

out of the handle for a wide letter. If the blade has not been adjusted to the width of the letter, you will find yourself cutting at a steeper angle which will make the letter too deep. A very wide letter will have a lesser angle of incision than a narrow letter.

The most significant advantage to using the mill knife is simplicity. Instead of having to decide on which of a variety of tools is needed to fit the various profiles of the letters, you need only one tool in your hand. Does it require a great deal of skill to master the mill knife? Using any carving tool takes hand-eye coordination and some practice. But with the one tool you can greatly limit the amount of practice time.

Another big advantage of the mill knife is speed. If you pit this tool against a router, and take into consideration the time it takes to set up sign-routing templates, you may find that the knife can do the same work in the same amount of time and the end result looks better.

Preparing the knife for use requires more than cutting down the blade to eliminate an end sticking out and poking you in the face. You also need to put bevels on the cutting edge. A bevel is the slope of the cutting edge, and you will need to put a bevel on each side of the blade. A double bevel allows you to turn the knife around in your hand and cut from either of its sides. If you do not have the equipment for beveling the knife blade, sharpening services are almost universally available.

ANGLE CUTS

Practice should begin with straight letters such as I and E, F and H. Since most of the lettering you will be doing will be narrow—less than 1" wide—you will be able to hold the knife at approximately 45 degrees to the wood. Dig the point of it into the wood at the top of one of these letters. In a continuous motion, draw or pull the knife down. If you make interrupted cuts instead, you will end up with multiple bevels and the bottom of the V will not be uniform.

To do the other side of the letter does not require moving to the top of the sign or turning the sign panel around. Try this technique: when you finish the down stroke, roll your wrist and hand over; return to the top of the letter, and pull the knife down again. This will take some practice, but the procedure will get you started for carving any style and size letter with the mill knife. When you have mastered the angle of the knife and the pulling motion, you will have uniformly v-shaped wedges of wood lifting up under your knife.

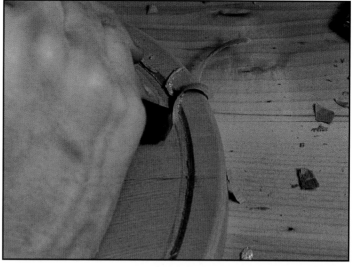

Use the mill knife to carve a v-groove as a border.

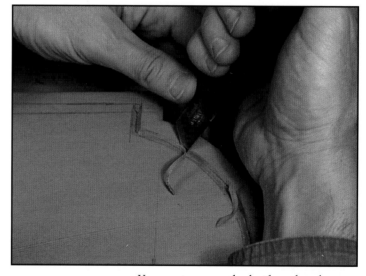

You must reverse the knife and push away to carve out the opposite side of the groove while following the grain.

Carving a vertical letter that follows the grain of the wood requires extra care because of subtle changes in grain direction. Such changes will cause the knife to drift or even split the wood rather than cut it.

RULES OF THE GRAIN

Those of us who work wood have an appreciation of grain direction. If you work a tool against the direction of grain, the result can be tear-out. This is the advice that goes with using a mill knife or any carving tool in wood: go with the direction of the grain. Whether you like it or not, the wood will dictate how it is to be carved.

To begin to understand how to carve an incised letter while dealing with the problems of grain direction, you need to look at how the letter flows with or against the grain. Take the letter O, for example, and divide it into four quadrants. Starting in the upper right quadrant if you are right-handed, on the outside of the letter just below the horizontal centerline, hold the knife at the angle you have practiced and push it away from you until you reach the top of the vertical centerline. To cut the inside of the letter, put the knife point at the top of the veritcal centerline, reverse the knife's direction, roll your fist over and pull it toward you until you reach the horizontal centerline. This procedure has the knife following the grain to make the incision and prevents grain tear-out.

For the lower right quadrant, do the outside of the letter first. Place the knife just above the horizontal centerline and pull it toward you until you reach the lower part of the vertical centerline. For the inside of the letter, reverse the knife, roll your fist over, put the point at the bottom of the vertical centerline and push it away from you until you reach the horizontal centerline. The entire process is reversed for the opposite half of the letter.

BREAKING THE RULES

On some letters, the rules of grain can be violated. On the letters V and W, for example, if you follow the grain you will be removing wood from one arm of the letter by working the knife down to its bottom, reversing the knife, and pushing it up on the opposite side of the arm. Wood grain is more forgiving when you are cutting across it than with it. For a V or a W, then, it is okay to cheat, meaning you can carve each side of these letters' arms starting at the tops of the letters.

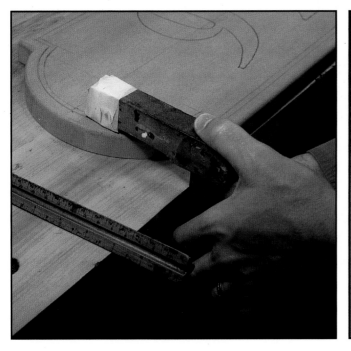

1. Before carving on the sign board, make sure it is securely clamped to the work surface. If you carve as suggested in the text, you will not have to move the sign.

2. When carving wood, you have to be aware that grain has direction. If you try carving against it, you will end up tearing, not carving out the wood. In the photo, the letter O has arrows that indicate the direction of the grain in the four quadrants of the letter. If you follow the arrows with the knife you end up with clean incisions.

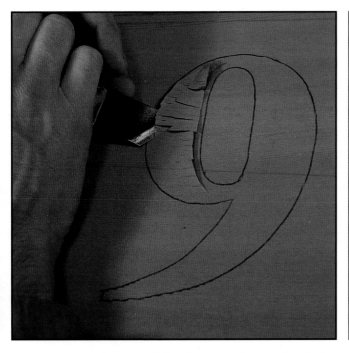

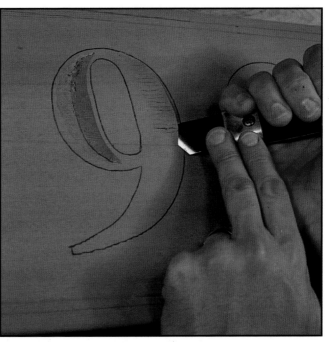

3. Letter carving begins with roughing out the wood with the mill knife. This means removing waste wood while not cutting to the outline of the letter.

4. With the wood roughed out from the left side, move to the lower right side and continue roughing out. Carving this way has the knife going with the grain to prevent tear-out. You can use the fingers of the opposite hand to act as a break to prevent the blade from leaving the outline of the letter.

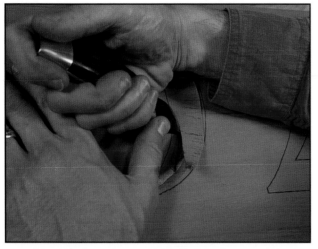

5. Pull the blade in the opposite direction on the opposite side of the letter. This technique has the knife following the grain. The opposite thumb helps push the blade and offers more control.

6. After roughing out, go back and carve to the outline.

7. More carving to the line. Push the knife away while using the thumb for extra control.

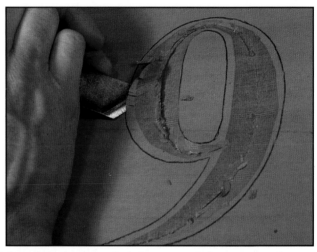

8. Pull the knife around the curve while cutting to the outline.

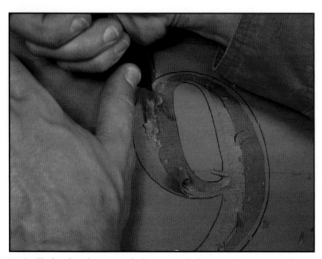

9. Pull the knife around the top of the number using the thumb for control.

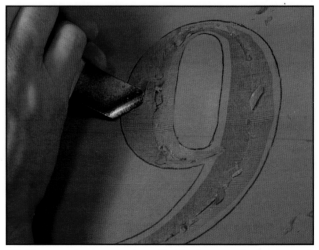

10. You may have to make a finished cut at the bottom of the v-shaped cut, especially if the letter is wide.

1. When cutting out vertical letters, as in this teak sign, simply pull the knife down from the top of the letter.

2. To carve the opposite side of the letter, roll your fist over and pull the blade down from the top.

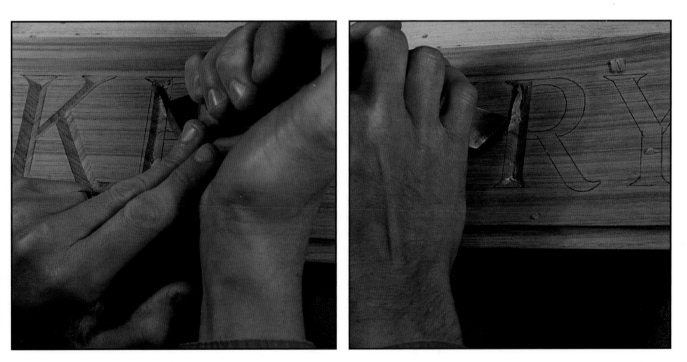

3. A finishing cut to the line.

4. A finished cut to the line on the opposite side of the letter.

55

5. Carving a serif, which is a corner of a letter.

6. Carving the top curve of the letter R. Notice how the knife follows the grain.

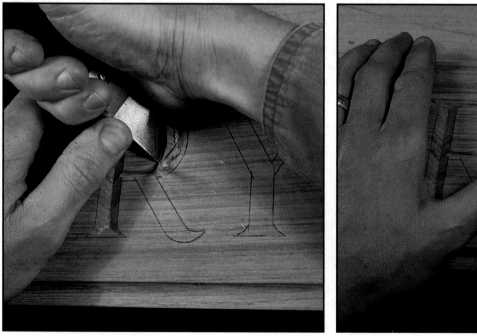

7. Carving the lower portion of the curve going in the opposite direction.

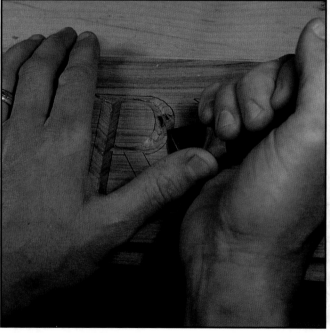

8. Carving the outside portion of the letter R.

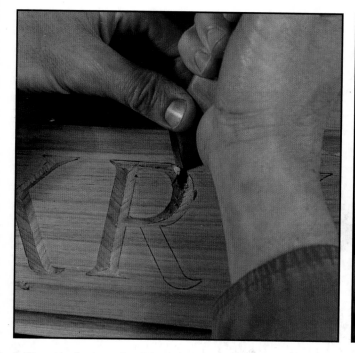

9. Carving the outside of the curve pushing the knife away while following the grain.

10. Roughing out the leg of the R.

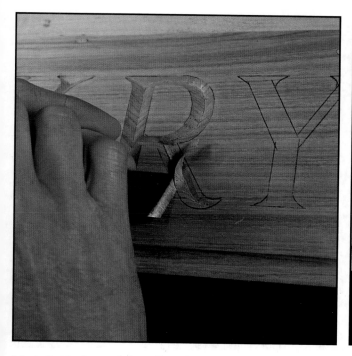

11. A finished cut while pulling the knife. Note how the wood comes up as wedges.

12. Pushing the knife away using the thumb of the opposite hand for control.

N

Serifs are the small lines used to finish off the main stroke of a letter. They vary in size and shape, and sometimes are not present at all, depending what type style you choose.

LETTER STYLES

Most beginning sign carvers start off with block letters. These have straight sides and tops that meet at right angles. But other lettering styles, such as Roman letters, have serifs. The Roman-style capital letter I, for example, has two sets of serifs, top and bottom. Serifs should present no problem because the mill knife point will negotiate the tightest turns. But you must check on the direction of the grain. It may be necessary to reverse the direction of the cut when incising a serif so that you are not going against the grain.

A HELPFUL THUMB

One hand holds the knife and does the cutting. This does not mean that your other hand cannot be put to use. The thumb of that hand can help guide and power your cuts. When pushing the blade on the upward cuts, the thumb can help push the blade from behind. As you pull your hand for the downward cuts, position the thumb at the front of the blade—not on the bevel—to help stop the blade from going beyond the bottom of the letter.

BLADE ADJUSTMENT

If you are working on letters of a consistent size, adjusting the blade is not necessary. But how do you know how far the blade should extend from its handle? There are no hard and fast rules for blade exposure. If the blade is not far enough out of the handle, and you are working on a wide letter, you will find yourself gripping the handle too far up, an uncomfortable way to control the knife. If the blade extends too far out and you are working on small letters, you will find your hand gripping the handle too close to the blade. To adjust the blade of any mill knife, simply loosen the set screw, pull the blade out or push it in, and tighten the screw.

AVOIDING STOP CUTS

Books and articles on sign carving letters often suggest making stop cuts down the centers of letters. This means pushing a chisel or gouge straight into the wood to "sink" a central line. The thinking behind this technique is that you need to know where the center of the letter is before you make your v-cuts.

Mastering the mill knife as an incision tool, holding it at the proper angle and making continuous pull or push strokes makes the centerline unnecessary. Not only does the centerline add extra and exacting work, but it also places an extra cut into the wood that may not be where your angled cuts meet.

Not all letters have to be done with a mill knife. Use a gouge to create a scalloped look. The wood pictured is mahogany.

The size of the gouge depends on the size of the letter. This tool is about 1" wide.

GOUGE CARVING

Not every letter, however, can be readily carved with just the mill knife. To carve very wide letters you may need the help of a gouge to remove wood more quickly and efficiently than a knife can handle. A gouge is also necessary when carving hardwoods such as oak, maple, walnut and cherry. Wood literally has to be chopped out with a gouge because the mill knife will not be able to remove more than a sliver of a very hard wood at a time.

When carving letters in a hardwood, you will need a gouge that has a number 3, 4 or 5 sweep. The sweep, with numbers that run from 2 to 11 in most cases, describes the profile or curve of the gouge. A number 3 gouge has a slight curve compared to the 11 gouge which is almost U-shaped.

The gouge, with the aid of a mallet, will chop out the wood from the inside of the letter and provide you with a cutting surface if you hold the tool at the same angle as you do with the knife. When gouging out a hardwood, start 1/16" inside of the letter line or as close as possible to the line. When you move on to incising the letters with a knife, you will find that you won't be able to remove more than a sliver of wood, especially if the wood is oak. If you need to chop out a very wide letter in a softwood like pine, start 1/8" in from the line. Softwoods are more forgiving than woods like oak, so you can remove that extra width of wood with the mill knife.

A gouge can replace the mill knife entirely. Many sign carvers use the gouge to create incisions that have a scalloped look to them. Though the scallops do not have the smooth look that the mill knife creates, the technique is especially effective when gold leafing the letters. The gold accentuates all those gouge cuts and makes for a striking effect.

1. When carving very wide letters, it is adviseable to chop out waste wood using a gouge.

2. A large gouge works well even when chopping out the wood in serifs.

3. The mill knife will clean up the ragged edges left by the gouge.

4. When working with a hardwood such as oak, you must chop out the waste wood with a gouge before using the mill knife.

ARNOLD BOCKLIN

A nice change of pace. Has an Art Deco look.

ABCDEFGHIJ
KLMNOPQRS
TUVWXYZ

abcdefghijklm
nopqrstuvwxyz

1234567890

""''!@#$%^&*()

A more informal script than Commercial Script

A B C D E F G H I J

K L M N O P Q R S

T U V W X Y Z

a b c d e f g h i j k l m

n o p q r s t u v w x y z

1 2 3 4 5 6 7 8 9 0

" " ' ! @ # $ % ^ & * ( )

Any Roman lettering style looks good carved.

ABCDEFGHIJ
KLMNOPQRS
TUVWXYZ

abcdefghijklm
nopqrstuvwxyz

1234567890

" " ' ! @ # $ % ^ & * ( )

Typical Roman style letter.

A B C D E F G H I J
K L M N O P Q R S
T U V W X Y Z

a b c d e f g h i j k l m
n o p q r s t u v w x y z
1 2 3 4 5 6 7 8 9 0
" " ' ' ! @ # $ % ^ & * ( )

A fancy letter that looks great carved.

A B C D E F G H I J

K L M N O P Q R S

T U V W X Y Z

a b c d e f g h i j k l m

n o p q r s t u v w x y z

1 2 3 4 5 6 7 8 9 0

" " ' ' ! @ # $ % & * ( )

A plain letter with slight serifs.

A B C D E F G H I J

K L M N O P Q R S

T U V W X Y Z

A B C D E F G H I J K L M

N O P Q R S T U V W X Y Z

1 2 3 4 5 6 7 8 9 0

" " ' ' ! @ # $ % ^ & * ( )

	SOME NOTES ON TYPE STYLES	
UPPER CASE:	Upper Case letters are more formal, bolder.
LOWER CASE:	Lower Case letters are more casual.
SCRIPT FONT:	Script looks fancier or more delicate.
SERIF:	Serifs are the small lines used to finish off the main stroke of a letter. They can be pointed, square or round.

A great style for carving. Looks great with wood finish.

A B C D E F G H I J

K L M N O P Q R S

T U V W X Y Z

a b c d e f g h i j k l m

n o p q r s t u v w x y z

1 2 3 4 5 6 7 8 9 0

" " ' ' ! @ # $ % ^ & * ( )

LETTERING STYLES

67

Block letters are easiest to carve.

ABCDEFGHIJ

KLMNOPQRS

TUVWXYZ

abcdefghijklm

nopqrstuvwxyz

1234567890

" " ' ' ! @ # $ % ^ & * ( )

GOUDY

A nice serif letter.

A B C D E F G H I J
K L M N O P Q R S
T U V W X Y Z

a b c d e f g h i j k l m
n o p q r s t u v w x y z

1 2 3 4 5 6 7 8 9 0

" " ' ' ! @ # $ % ^ & * ( )

SANS SERIF:	Sans Serif letters have no serif. Block letters are san serif, have a plain look and are easy to read.
ITALIC TYPE:	Italic type leans to the right.
CONDENSED:	Condensed type is made taller. Usually makes letters appear narrow.

SOME NOTES ON TYPE STYLES

Slightly more contemporary than other serif letters.

PARK AVENUE

A very elegant letter.

A B C D E F G H I J

K L M N O P Q R S

T U V W X Y Z

a b c d e f g h i j k l m

n o p q r s t u v w x y z

1 2 3 4 5 6 7 8 9 0

" " ' ' ! @ # $ % ^ & * ( )

Makes you think of the circus.

ABCDEFGHIJ

KLMNOPQRS

TUVWXYZ

abcdefghijklm

nopqrstuvwxyz

1234567890

""'!@#$%^&*()

SWISS HELVETICA

One variation of a sans serif letter.

ABCDEFGHIJ

KLMNOPQRS

TUVWXYZ

abcdefghijklm

nopqrstuvwxyz

1 2 3 4 5 6 7 8 9 0

" " ' ' ! @ # $ % ^ & * ( )

Has a few nice flairs on some serifs.

ABCDEFGHIJ
KLMNOPQRS
TUVWXYZ

abcdefghijklm
nopqrstuvwxyz

1234567890

"",''!@#$%^&*()

WINDSOR ELONGATED

A good style to use if you want tall condensed letters.

A B C D E F G H I J

K L M N O P Q R S

T U V W X Y Z

a b c d e f g h i j k l m

n o p q r s t u v w x y z

1 2 3 4 5 6 7 8 9 0

" " ' ' ! @ # $ % ^ & * ( )

ITC ZAPF CHANCERY

The lower case letters have a nice look.

A B C D E F G H I
J K L M N O P Q R S
T U V W X Y Z
a b c d e f g h i j k l m
n o p q r s t u v w x y z
1 2 3 4 5 6 7 8 9 0
" " ' ' ! @ # $ % ^ & * ( )

CHAPTER FIVE

APPLIQUES AND RELIEF CARVING

The trend today is to have a sign that offers more than lettering. It may incorporate a logo into its design or something personal. A family that enjoys sailing may desire a sailboat as part of a house sign. A hunter may want a pheasant as a feature of his name sign. The most common approach is to add a piece of carved design or applique.

An applique, or applied panel of wood, needs the same treatment as the sign panel. If it is cut from a single piece of wood, the wood needs to be as flat as possible. If the applique is large and has to be glued up, the boards need to be joined carefully and sanded flat. And if the applique is to be part of an exterior sign, it must be glued to the panel with a waterproof glue.

Designs for appliques can be transferred using carbon paper onto a piece of wood. A bandsaw is the best tool for cutting out the shape of a small applique, although large ones will require the sabersaw. But the problem with an applique is whether to carve it before it is glued down to the panel or after it is glued in place.

Appliques or added pieces of carved wood are attractive additions to signs as is the case with this pheasant.

A falcon applique on a public school sign.

An oyster shell applique on a community sign.

Three pumpkins applied to a grocery store sign.

Design will dictate whether to carve before or after the glue-down. A restaurant, for example, wants a lobster as part of its sign. The lobster design has thin or narrow legs. This is an applique that should be glued down and then carved. It is too difficult to carve the fragile legs and then transfer the cutout to the sign panel. A sporting goods store wants a basketball as part of the sign. This is an easy applique because rounding over the cutout will put little stress on the wood, which can be carved and then applied.

SECURING THE APPLIQUE

Whether you carve the applique before the glue-down or after it has been glued in place, you should secure it with fasteners. Drywall screws through a piece of plywood, which is then clamped to a bench, will do the trick when working on the applique separate from the sign panel. But you have to be careful not to have the screws penetrate the face of the wood or extend close to the surface. Hitting a screw will ruin the edge of the carving tool.

GLUING DOWN THE APPLIQUE

Before gluing the applique to the sign panel, you want to be sure of its location. Once that is determined, you will have to outline it in pencil. This obviously locates it, but it also gives you a zone for putting screws through the sign to secure the applique. Screws serve two purposes. They help clamp the applique to the panel while the glue is setting up. They also secure the applique in the event the glue should fail in the future.

Once you have decided where to place the screws, you want to drill screw holes slightly smaller in diameter than the screw, from the face of the sign through to the back, leaving an exit hole. Then thread the screws in from the back until about 1/8" protrudes through the front of the sign panel. Next position the applique above its outline on the panel and press it down on the screw points. When you remove the applique you will have located where you want to pre-drill for the screws.

It is important to have a good bond between the applique and the panel. You want both pieces of wood covered with glue—not too thin and not too thick. If the glue is too thin you will not get a good bond; if too thick there will be too much glue squeeze-out.

A flush fit is also important. If your sign is to go outdoors, you do not want water getting between the applique and panel. It can rot the wood over time. And in climates where water freezes, the freezing and thawing action may crack the applique, regardless of the glue used.

To encourage a flush fit, you want the screws just long enough to grip the applique, yet not protrude through its surface. You also do not want the screw too near a surface that is going to be carved. A 1" thick applique should have no more than 1/2" of the screw protruding through the front of the sign. Thicker appliques can have longer screws.

It is best not to use an electric drill with a screw driver bit to tighten up the screws. Too much force may damage the back of the sign or drive the screw too far into the applique, particularly when using a softwood like redwood. Put the drill aside and use a screwdriver.

CLAMPING AN APPLIQUE

The combination of screws and a good bonding agent like WEST System®, is all you will need for gluing down most appliques. But clamping is often recommended. This is difficult if the sign is large and the applique is somewhere in the middle of a wide expanse of wood. Most shop clamps, unfortunately, cannot extend more than a few inches into a board.

Sign carvers have developed some interesting strategies to deal with the problem of clamping appliques. One is to clamp down the applique using heavy lumber: 4x4s in softwood, 2x2s in hardwood. By laying the

A bouquet of flowers applied to a florist shop sign.

The bandsaw is ideal for cutting out most appliques.

The wood baseball hat, shaped and sanded with power tools, is large enough to be hand-held when worked on. The hat will become part of a sign for a sports memorabilia store.

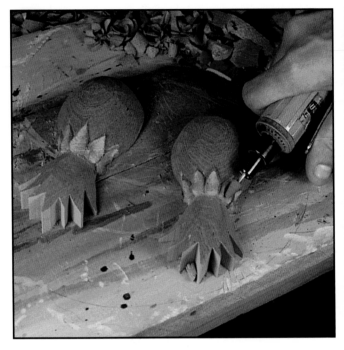

1. Appliques can either be carved separately from the sign and then glued in placed or glued down and then carved. These two pineapples are secured to a board and worked on with an air-powered tool.

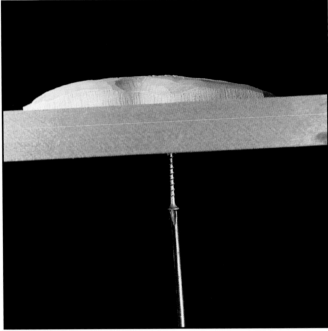

2. An applique must be secured to a sign with glue, but screws holding it from the back of the sign will replace the need for clamps. The screws also hold the applique in place should the glue fail in the future.

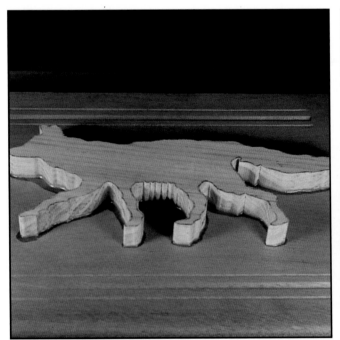

3. A glued-down applique of a fox ready to be carved.

4. A fishtail gouge is excellent for most applique carving.

5. The fishtail is turned over to give a rounded shape to the applique.

6. Use the mill knife to remove glue squeezed out between the applique and the sign.

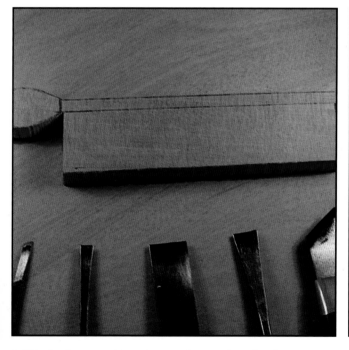

7. The backsaw applique is part of a sign for a lumber company. Surrounding it are the five carving tools that will be used to carve it, including gouges and a mill knife.

8. Carving away wood with a fishtail gouge.

9. Handsanding the applique.

10. A more detailed applique of leaves for a dentist's sign, glued down and ready to be carved with the eight tools pictured.

11. An explosion of chips made with just a gouge, which removes much of the wood when rounding the applique.

12. A very pointed knife puts in the leaf veins.

boards—which should be slightly longer than the width of the sign—across the top of the applique and across the bottom of the sign panel, the ends of these boards can then be clamped with pipe clamps. If the boards are positioned across only the top of the applique, there is a risk of cracking either the sign or the applique because of uneven pressure.

Another strategy is the use of the vacuum bag system. This method requires that pieces being glued together be put in a flexible vinyl bag. When air is pumped out of the bag, the atmospheric pressure acts like a giant clamp with almost perfect distribution of force.

Tools for carving a sign with dolphin ends and a rope border.

DEALING WITH GLUE SQUEEZE-OUT

If you plan on painting your sign, glue squeeze-out, the inevitable result of clamping an applique, is not so critical. Little or no glue squeeze-out indicates that not enough glue was applied. Glue becomes a problem when you want to stain the sign board. The glue will not allow the stain to penetrate the wood.

To remedy the problem, wait for the squeezed-out glue to dry. Attempting to remove it when it is still wet will only smear the glue around and enlarge the area that cannot be stained. Squeezed-out glue when dry will most probably be in the form of beads. The beads can be removed with a chisel or a small file. But you have to be careful not to gouge the wood. Sanding out the gouges is exceptionally difficult around an applique.

TOOLS FOR MAKING APPLIQUES

One of the most useful tools for rounding over an applique, which means giving it a three-dimensional look, is the fishtail gouge. The fishtail has a straight blade that flares out as it nears the cutting edge. The advantage of this gouge is that it can get into tight areas; it is also lighter and easier to use than a gouge that is wide along its entire length. You can use the fishtail with a mallet for hardwoods or with just your hands for softwoods. A number 3 fishtail about 3/4" wide will handle small and large appliques.

You do not need many more tools to do simple appliques. A v-parting tool with its two cutting edges will cut channels into the wood, but the mill knife will do the same job. In fact, it would be useful to develop some carving techniques using the knife to cut out shapes and even round over wood. A skew chisel, much favored by professional carvers, will also work well.

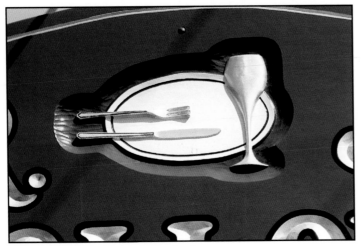

Relief carving means removing background so that an area can stand out. The table setting was relief-carved for a restaurant.

Other tools that can be used for appliques are files, rasps and rifflers, all of which have teeth that cut. Sanding devices such as sanding drums chucked up in a drill will help with more aggressive wood removal, shaping and even finishing.

RELIEF CARVING

Relief carving is a form of carving that raises a design by clearing away the background. The simplest relief carving can be done with the mill knife. You make a series of v-shaped cuts, as you would do for an incised letter, to outline an object and put some detail into its interior. Though this technique is not as sculptural as other forms of carving, the results will look much like incised letters. If you gold leaf the v-cuts, the effect will be striking.

More typical of relief carving is removing most of the background so that the design stands out from its background. A router with a straight bit is the best choice for effectively removing wood both quickly and at a uniform depth. The combination of power and cutting action is not intimidated by grain direction. The tool will remove quantities of wood from any direction.

Though straight bits range in size from $1/8"$ to $1 1/4"$ in diameter, the preferred choice is the $1/4"$ bit. The bit will not put a strain on the router nor will it remove too much wood around the design. For getting into very small, tight areas the $1/8"$ diameter bit is useful.

To raise up a sign design or logo you do not have to remove the entire background. An oval of wood removed around the design often creates the most pleasing effect. The router can do this effectively, but handtools are still needed to break down the wall of wood left by the straight bit. A gouge will create a slope from the surface of the sign panel to the bottom of the raised design. The gouge will also remove irregularities left by the bit. Not a lot of work is required with the gouge since the depth has been predetermined by the setting of the bit.

Although the router is efficient and fast in removing background, it can run into a problem when it reaches an edge of the raised area if so much background has been removed that there is not enough support for the base of the router. The router will have a tendency to tip over and the bit will dig too deeply into the background.

A solution is to replace the baseplate of the router with a larger plate, preferrably a square one. You can make your own baseplate using a $1/4"$ thick Lucite. The plastic material drills easily and allows you to see the entire panel surface. There is no limit as to how big to make the plastic baseplate. But it should be large enough so that the router will not tip over into removed background.

The same tools used to round over the applique can be used to round over a relief design. Gouges, especially the fishtail, will gently remove wood down to the background while a v-parting tool or a mill knife can carve in narrow lines or separations. Other gouges with different sweeps may be necessary to enhance the contours of the design.

To Apply or Relief?

Sign carvers may debate whether to apply a design or carve it into the panel. Degree of difficulty is part of the problem. While many think that an applique does more to emphasize the design, more work is involved. Some carvers will design a sign so that the design is both relieved and carved. This means both routing out the background and adding an applique to the sign panel. The effect of the added wood creates a three-dimensional look that is dramatic.

Cutouts

Occasionally sign carvers will create some negative or blank space in the interior of a sign by making cutouts. This allows some feature of the sign to be admired while there is an open area around some or all of the design. Cutouts can even accentuate an applique or a relieved area. But cutouts are usually done on signs suspended from or mounted on posts since putting the sign on a wall would defeat the purpose of having empty space.

When doing cutouts, more care has to be taken if dowels or biscuits have been used so that they do not show themselves when wood is removed. The best tool for making cutouts is the saber saw. By simply drilling a hole into the area to be cut out, you can put the blade of the saw into it and easily remove the wood.

Whichever you choose—the relief, the applique, cutouts, or even a melding of all three—make sure you are comfortable with the tools you have available. Be certain you can handle a router comfortably and exercise the appropriate caution with a tool that has a bit spinning at 25,000 rpm. Keep your work surfaces clear of clutter, your extension cords out of the way, and make sure your tools are sharp.

Much of your sharpening can be done using a belt sander and a 100 grit belt.

You need to go to a buffing wheel to put a fine edge on the tool you sharpened on the belt sander.

SHARPENING

Incised letters should never have to be sanded unless they are very wide. A well-sharpened tool pushed or pulled with a continuous motion should leave a smooth wall in the woods recommended. Even scalloped letters are best done with a well-honed gouge. Sharpening is as critical as any other technique or tool for sign carving.

Many sharpening tools and systems are available to woodworkers. They include stones, leather strops, and grinding wheels. Most of your sharpening, however, can be done using the same tool you use for sanding—the belt sander.

When using an electric grinding wheel, there is always the problem of burning the steel of your tool. This results in a blue edge that loses its strength or temper. When sharpening on a wheel you need to keep the steel wet. Sharpening on stones requires oil as a lubricant, but the procedure is slow. The belt sander does just as effective a job with less water dousing and is quicker than a sharpening stone.

By clamping down a belt sander so that the belt is facing up, you have a grinding tool. For most sharpening use 100 or 120 grit sanding belts. A coarser grit puts too many scratches into the steel and a finer grit will wear out too quickly and may burn the steel before you realize it. You must still dip the end of your tool into water, but the newer the belt you are using, the less dousing is required.

When holding the tool to the revolving belt, move the blade back and forth. If you hold the blade in one place for too long you risk distorting the bevel and heating up the steel too quickly. What you want is a continuous bevel with a slight burr or rounding over on the end. You can feel the burr with your fingers, and until you have a burr on the end, the tool has not been sharpened sufficiently.

To remove the burr you will need a motor-powered buffing wheel made from cotton or felt. For the buffing wheel to efficiently take away that burr while at the same time polishing the bevel, you have to apply a polishing compound. A semi-hard compound, polishing compound comes in stick form and it is pushed into the wheel as it is spinning. The rouge comes in different grits, each having its own color. Red seems to work best for most carving needs. The combination of the rouge and the spinning cotton wheel will quickly take away the burr and polish the bevel.

1. The sailboat was relief-carved on a separate board, which was added to the sign.

2. The flowers were relief-carved for a dentist's sign.

3. The windmill was carved on a separate panel for a condominium sign.

4. Use a router with a straight bit to remove wood from around an area that is to be relieved.

5. The mill knife squares up the outline left by the router. Use a gouge to clean up the router marks and give the sign a hand-carved look.

6. Use the mill knife for detail carving.

Carving a Ribbon Board

Because of the influence of naval law that ships identify themselves, signboards on a boat's stern or quarters are popular. The quarterboard style is also a popular choice for house and commercial signs. One of the most appealing styles is the ribbon board, called that because of its folded and split ends that suggest a swallowtail.

A good design for a ribbon board has a double fold at each end. This means that the ribbon folds under itself, drops down, flattens out, then folds back up and continues to its split ends. To make this ribbon board you will need a saw, a gouge with a fairly flat shape (a no. 3 being ideal) and a sanding attachment such as a drum sander.

After you have cut the board to shape—an 8/4 board offers good thickness—and sanded it smooth, turn the board on its side and determine how deep you want the area between the two folds to be. This will be a flattened area lower than the surface of the sign. To remove wood down to that level, you need to make stop cuts where the folds of the ribbon are. You can use either a handsaw or a hand-held circular saw with its blade set to the correct depth.

Next use the gouge with a mallet to remove wood to the depth of the saw cuts. The gouge will also make stop cuts where the ribbon fans out below its bottom profile. You also want to give some shape to the ribbon as it works its way out to the swallowtail split. Draw a curving profile on the edge to create the effect of a slightly wavy surface. The profile does not have to be very deep to create this effect. Take the gouge and chop away wood down to that profile. You can carve across the grain as well as with it.

To duplicate the folded-under look, you will have to carve three levels of wood. One is the top of the ribbon. The next is the fold. The third is the lower plane of the ribbon. This stepped-down look can be done with a gouge, and you can use the gouge to make stop cuts. Then use the tool to flatten out the levels.

Sanding the various levels smooth is the last step. You can use either hand-held sandpaper or a sanding drum in a drill. Power sanding is definitely preferred for hardwoods.

1. A circular saw quickly establishes the different levels or sets the depth of the ribbon where it folds.

2. Use a gouge to shape the folds.

3. Use a mill knife to cut straight down around the ribbon folds.

4. Use a large gouge against the grain to create a ruffled look on the ribbon ends.

5. Remove wood with the gouge going with the grain.

6. Though many sanding devices are available, a quick and efficient way to remove gouge marks is with a drum sander in a power drill.

CHAPTER SIX

FINISHING AND GOLD LEAFING

Leaving a sign unfinished is rarely, if ever, an option. Wood, even if kept indoors, needs a chemical sealant to preserve it from the damage of light. If the wood is stained to enhance the grain, it surely needs varnish or polyurethane to seal it and keep the stain fresh looking. And if you apply paint, you are giving the wood stronger protection as well as color.

BRUSHES

Finishing begins with the right brush. There are two kinds of brushes available: natural bristle brushes for oil paints and varnishes, and nylon bristles for latex paints.

Avoid using the wrong brush. A natural bristle brush, for example, should never be used with latex paints. Also, buy the most expensive brush you can find among the natural and nylon bristle brushes. The better brushes will last longer, give you a better finish, clean up more easily, and have a better feel.

Many sign carvers and painters use brushes with round handles. These allow the painter to spin out the thinner used for cleaning. After taking the brush out of the paint thinner, transfer it to a small cardboard box and literally spin the brush and beat it against the sides of the box until the thinner is gone. In the painting trade this is known as a beat box. You can also purchase a brush spinner.

Because brushes come in different widths, you may find it difficult to know what size to use. As a rule of thumb for signs measuring 8' or longer and at least 3' wide, a 2 1/2" wide brush will be most practical. For signs measuring 4' to 8' and approximately 2' wide, a 2" brush is best. And for small signs under 4' long and 1' wide, a 1" or 2" wide brush will suffice.

Rollers are out of the question for sign painting. A roller leaves not only too thin a coat, but it also cannot get the paint into carved or incised wood.

LETTERING QUILLS

Brushes for painting lines or applying the adhesive for gold leaf are called lettering quills. These brushes have bristles about 1" long and come in sizes from 0 to 28. The smallest size can produce a line about 3/32" wide, while the largest makes a line about 3/4" wide. Lettering quills are indispensible to sign painters, but they are not inexpensive. It would be worthwhile to invest in several of the smaller sizes for your sign work.

CARING FOR THE BRUSHES

Professional sign painters store their brushes, but not quills, in thinner. Every time a brush dries out, no matter how well it may have been spun and beaten, it stiffens up and continues to do so with each cleaning. If storing your brushes in thinner is not practical, here is some advice to follow. First, squeeze out the paint or varnish onto a paper towel. Squeezing removes about 75 percent of the paint or varnish. Then soak the brush in paint or lacquer thinner—the latter useful for pigmented products such as oil paints. Make sure the bristles are completely covered by the thinner. Never put paint and varnish brushes in the same cleaning container. When cleaning, it is important not to have the brush standing up on its bristles. When you do this to a brush you distort the hairs. The effect is called "fishtailing." To suspend the brush in cleaner, use an empty coffee can with a plastic lid. Cut a hole in the lid that is slightly smaller than the the handle. With the brush handle wedged into the hole, it will hang suspended in the thinner.

Lettering quills require as much if not more care than brushes. Since it is very easy to distort these bristles, quills should never be

Wood must be primed if it is to be painted. Shown is a white oil-based primer applied to a redwood sign.

allowed to stand in a jar or can of thinner. Neither should the quills be stored in thinner. Instead, they should be cleaned two or three times and then stored where the bristles will not be distorted. The best advice here is to keep them flat and away from dust.

PRIMING AND PAINTING

There are many paint products available to the sign carver, from primers to oil paints to latex. Most everyone has used latex to paint a room or exterior siding. It applies easily and dries quickly. It is also easy to clean a latex brush with just soap and water. But bubbling

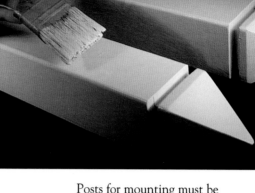

Posts for mounting must be treated the same way as the sign. At least two coats of primer are needed as shown in the photo.

can be a problem with dried latex. This is caused when moisture on a humid day gets into the paint. When the paint has dried, it may bubble up and blister. In fact, bubbling occasionally occurs with oil paints as well.

Oil paints dry slower but flow on the wood more smoothly than latex. Oil paints also bond better to wood fibers. Whichever paint you choose, you must first prime the wood.

If the sign is an exterior one, apply at least two coats of primer, whether latex or oil. Three coats are recommended for signs facing south into the sun. Building up a finish is essential for exterior signs. The harshness of the sun, rain, freezing and pollution all take their toll.

Some woods such as redwood and cedar do not accept latex easily. These must be sealed with an oil-based primer.

Apply paint over the primer using a wide brush if the sign is large. The bristle brush measures 2$\frac{1}{2}$".

After the primer has dried, apply the paint. One coat of paint is never enough for a sign. For a sign with a southern exposure, use a minimum of three or four coats of paint. A sign facing north and away from the sun holds up well with three coats. Signs facing west may also need four coats, especially if the sun is especially strong in the afternoon. Signs facing east should get at least three coats of paint.

There are basic painting techniques to keep in mind. When painting, brush on even coats that are not too heavy or too thin. Make consistent, back-and-forth strokes, and watch out for drips. Check over the entire sign before putting the brush away.

Use a small paint brush to remove puddles of varnish in the letters.

With the aid of a computer-generated template you seal the letters without getting size or paint on the background, which already has a finish. The template takes the guesswork out of painting or gold-leafing letters.

DEPUDDLING PAINT

Priming or painting a flat surface is not too challenging, but problems can arise when dealing with incised letters. If paint puddles at the bottoms of the carved letters, it means that too much paint has flowed into the valleys. Some minor puddling is necessary because the areas of incised or carved-out wood soak up finish more readily than the surface wood. More rather than less primer and paint is needed in the letters. However, an excess means puddles, which can be wicked up with a disposable brush.

CONDITIONERS

Sign painters and house and commercial painters usually add conditioners to their paints. These are chemicals that help the paint come off the brush more easily, make the paint flow better, and even help with drying.

Two common conditioners, available at most paint and hardware stores, are Penetrol® and Floetrol®. For oil-based paints, Penetrol® is recommended; for latex paints, use Floetrol®. It is best to add the conditioner when first opening the can of paint. The recommended mix of conditioner is about 10 percent of the paint volume.

FINISHING TIPS

It is always a good technique to sand between coats; 220 grit is the best to use for paint or varnish. Any paper that is coarser will scratch the finish. When using sandpaper, use a light touch. Too much pressure removes the paint. If you want to use hand-held sandpaper, fold a piece 3$^{1}/_{2}$" wide by 11" long into thirds. This gives the paper some stiffness. You can also use a sanding block, but make sure it is rubber so that there is some give. A wood sanding block is too hard on the finish.

A tack cloth—cheese cloth soaked in varnish to make it sticky—will do an effective job of removing sanding dust. If you rub too hard with the cloth, however, you risk leaving some of the sticky varnish on the surface, making it difficult for the next coat of finish to adhere. The trick is to wipe, not rub. Vacuuming immediately after each sanding also helps to remove dust and keep the tack cloth from getting clogged.

FINISHING FRONT AND BACK

There is no reason why you cannot paint both the front, back and edges of a sign when applying each coat. One technique is to lay the back of the sign on the points of nails that have been driven through a board. Do this immediately after painting the back. The sign will look like it is sitting on a bed of nails, but contact is minimal and the nails will not puncture the wood. Another strategy is to drive screws partially into the ends of the sign. The sign can then hang suspended on the screws when placed between saw horses.

Still another technique for making minimal contact between a work surface and the sign uses triangulated strips of wood. Nail them to the sawhorses so that a point of each triangle sticks up. Lay the sign across the strips and you have a sturdy support that will have minimal effect on the paint.

STAINS AND VARNISHES

So many brands of wood stains are on the market, it is difficult for most consumers to know what to buy. For a sign, particularly one going outdoors, limit your choices by purchasing an exterior stain. Most brands come in different consistencies, ranging from transparent to semi-transparent to high-hiding, the last having the look of a flat paint. The best choices for signs are the first two consistencies.

Stains can be brushed or wiped onto the surface of the wood. Apply one or two coats with a brush, wiping each one with a piece of lint-free cloth. The stain should leave a deep, rich tone with the grain showing through. If you want to test the color of the stain on the wood, try a sample area on the back of the sign.

Stained wood needs a clear coating to preserve and seal it. Polyurethanes and varnishes are the choices. For outdoor signs, exterior polyurethanes and varnishes are readily available. Be aware that most exterior clear coatings leave a glossy finish. For interior signs, you have the option of choosing satin or semi-gloss finishes. Before applying the coating, mix in a conditioner—Penetrol® is recommended—using about 10 percent to the volume.

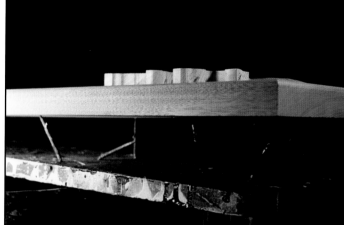

Both sides of a sign can be painted during each coat. Paint the back of the sign, put it on this bed of nails, and paint the front. The nail points have little effect on the paint and they will not penetrate the wood if you do not press down on it.

Three two-sided signs are held with screws and support boards on both ends. Temporarily suspending a sign this way allows you to paint both sides in a single operation because you can flip the assembly over on the saw horses.

Stained signs that will be displayed out of doors require an exterior varnish and a bristle brush. Shown is a teak boat sign. Always "wash" teak with lacquer thinner before applying varnish.

Hand sand lightly between coats of varnish using 220-grit sandpaper. Then use a tack cloth to remove excess dust.

The big difference between a clear coating and paint is the durability. Varnishes and polyurethanes last about two-thirds as long as a painted finish. They may not prevent the wood from fading due to exposure to sunlight, and they tend eventually to peel under harsh sunlight. Clear coatings require more applications than paint. Consider that a boat with wood trim may have up to 30 coats of varnish applied to the wood before it leaves the factory. For an exterior sign you should apply at least six coats of varnish or polyurethane.

After each coat of finish, check for drips, missed spots and foreign objects. Hair, dust and especially bugs are all problems when painting. One moth fluttering across a wet surface can ruin the finish and make it impossible to touch up.

GOLD LEAFING

Gold leaf gives brilliance to incised letters or carving, and it usually lasts for decades out-of-doors. In fact, you need not even have carved letters or logos for the gold leaf to be effective. It can be applied to a flat wood surface—much as it is done on glass doors, fire and rescue vehicles.

Gilders, as they were traditionally called, applied gold leaf to furniture, ornamental objects and picture frames. The technique was particularly popular during the Renaissance, but today, due to the cost, gilding or gold leafing is seldom done on wood, with the exception of signs.

Gold leaf is real gold that is sold by the book, the pack or in rolls. A book of gold contains 25 very thin leaves or sheets of gold. A pack consists of 20 books containing a total of 500 leaves of gold.

Gold leaf has a standard size of $3\,3/8$" by $3\,3/8$". A book of gold leaf will cover about $1\,1/2$ square feet. A pack will cover about 30 square feet.

Gold leaf comes in several varieties. The purest is 24 karat gold. Most sign carvers prefer 23 karat gold XXDeep gold leaf because of its permanence outdoors. Gold leaf is available in 22 karat, but contains more alloy than the 23 karat gold, and the leaf eventually tarnishes when exposed to the weather.

Gold leaf is also available in rolls. Rolls 67 feet in length come in widths of ¹/₈" to 3¹/₄". Rolls are used extensively for striping and incised letters.

PREPARING THE SURFACE FOR GOLD LEAFING

Gold leaf cannot be applied to raw wood. The wood must first be sealed. Gold leaf can and should be put down over primer and paint or over stain and varnish. What holds the gold to the surface is "size," an adhesive base. Never seal the gold after it's been applied; sealer will dull the gold.

Gilders who still apply gold leaf to frames and furniture use a process called water gilding. This means they apply the gold to a colored background consisting of a clay mixed with a glue. The glue is the binding agent—much like size—and can be reactivated with water to hold the gold to the clay. However, to gold leaf a sign, use oil size.

Oil size comes in a quick- as well as a slow-setting size. The slow-setting size is the better choice. You have more working time with it, usually 3 to 4 hours depending on the climate. When using quick-setting size the gold will not come out as shiny as with slow-setting size.

The biggest problem with gold-leaf size, which should never be diluted with a paint thinner, is judging when it is dry enough for the gold to adhere properly. Size that is too wet will cause the gold leaf to "drown" and appear dull. If the size is too dry, the gold leaf will not adhere and the resulting coverage will be spotty.

Slow-setting size can take anywhere from 12 to 36 hours before it is ready for the gold. One way to insure that the size dries in a consistent manner is to make sure you stir the can of size. If you do neglect to stir it, the size will take much longer to dry.

Gold-leaf size will also dry differently on different finishes. It will take longer to dry on

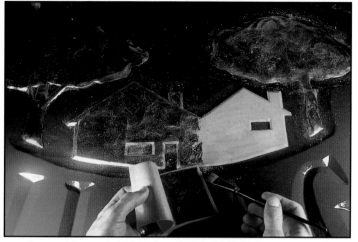

Applying a sheet of gold leaf to a relieved logo.

Gold leaf can also be applied to such sign accessories as post finials.

Test the tackiness of gold-leaf size with a knuckle. Keep a record of when the size was applied.

97

The computer template makes sizing a letter easy. It is impossible to get the size outside the letter when the template is in place. Keep the template in position while you apply the gold leaf, and when you peel away the template there will be no clean-up needed around the letters.

latex than on oil paint, for example. Gold leafing is not a casual operation. You literally have to schedule your time around the drying process, although applying size in the evening and waiting until the next day is a good strategy to follow.

To determine when the size is ready for the application of the gold leaf, try testing its tackiness not with a finger but with your knuckle. If the size is not dry enough, it will feel sticky. It may even come off on your skin. You will then need to wait. If it is too dry, you will feel no stickiness at all. In that case, you will have to start over and resize the area.

If you are working with gold leaf for the first time, it may pay you to try some test strips. This requires applying the size to a surface similar to the sign you are gilding. Simply paint a series of lines of size on the surface, make a note of the time, and apply gold leaf to the first stripe after at least 10 hours. Wait an hour and apply gold leaf to the next stripe and so on. Be aware that humidity and air temperature are both factors in how long it takes for the size to dry.

When applying size, it is important to make sure it is applied only to the surfaces to be gold-leafed. The application takes some skill and a steady hand. If you get size on the surface of the sign and you do not remove it, gold will stick to the unwanted size later on. Size can be removed by gently wiping a rag slightly dampened with paint thinner over the area.

To apply size, you should use a good quality lettering quill. The brush will make a good straight or curved line with an even stroke. Since the bristles of a lettering quill are long, they will hold a good deal of size.

A discarded glossy magazine works nicely as a palette when applying the size. Tear off the top sheet and let the inside pages be your palette. Drip puddles of size about 1" in diameter onto the paper and load up the lettering quill from the puddle. If too much size gets on the brush, you can spin out some of the size on a dryer part of the page.

APPLYING THE GOLD

Many people think that gold leaf is painted on. Actually it is pushed off the sheet of paper to which it adheres slightly and onto the sized surface. A brush does the pushing, gravity lets it fall onto the size, and the size does the bonding.

To apply the gold, you will need a good sable brush. Soft yet firm, the sable brush will not scratch the metal and it will break apart a sheet of gold leaf easily. Many sign carvers use a gilder's tip made of soft camel's hair. Even the best bristle brush will not do an effective job moving the gold off the paper onto the size. Nor will it gently break apart a sheet of gold. Being able to break away only part of a sheet is important to keep from wasting the gold. If only a small area is to be gold leafed, you do not need an entire sheet to do it.

ROLLS VS. LEAVES

Sheets of gold leaf cannot be cut with scissors. Instead, they must be broken apart gently with the brush to avoid wasting gold. This takes some skill. The solution for working narrow areas such as letters or borders and edges is the rolled gold, which can be applied with more accuracy and less waste than sheets. When applying rolled gold to wide, incised letters, it is best to lay down a strip on each slope or side of the letter, not across the entire letter. By attempting to cover a wide letter all at once, the result may be incomplete coverage and a cracking in the gold's surface.

Sheet gold has its advantages. When doing a large area such as a carved relief or applique, the sheet is indispensible for its coverage. You can literally drape a sheet of gold over the area.

Whichever you choose, rolls or sheets, the wood must be finished properly—free of dust and imperfections—otherwise the gold leaf will serve to accentuate those problems.

Rolled gold is very useful when doing borders.

Applying oil-based slow-drying size, an adhesive for gold leaf, with a lettering quill.

Applying ¹/₂" wide roll of 23 karat gold leaf.

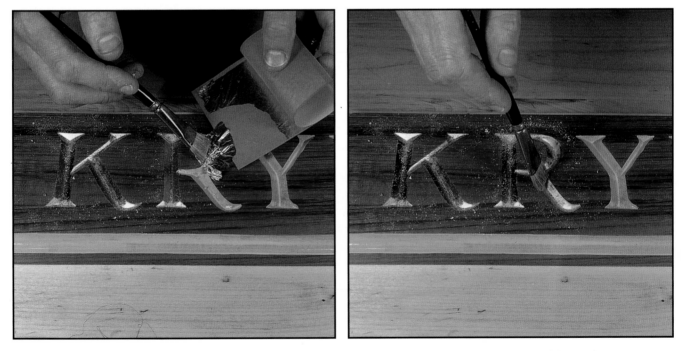

Where the rolled gold will not turn in a circular letter, use gold taken from a sheet. Gold leaf comes in sheets that measure 3 ³/₈" by 3 ³/₈". Use a red sable brush to break away some of the gold from the sheet and push it into the letter.

Use the red sable brush to push the gold into the size.

Use a sable brush to push the gold onto the border.

Use a slightly wet cotton ball to burnish the gold.

BURNISHING THE GOLD

Burnishing, or polishing, the gold is done with a ball of cotton, slightly wetted with water and squeezed out. Dry cotton will scratch the gold. Burnishing accomplishes several things. First, it improves the bond by pushing the gold into the size. Second, it removes wrinkles caused by the gold piling up on the size. And third, burnishing gives a nice shine to the gold.

MORE TIPS ON GOLD LEAFING

Gold leaf, though durable outdoors, is not meant to be touched. Putting your fingers on the gold will smudge it. When burnishing, do not rub too hard. Instead, use the cotton in a gentle wiping motion. And never seal the gold with a clear finish. Not only is it unnececssary, but it may dull the gold.

Cleanup is also important because particles of gold leaf will adhere to the background of the signboard. A rag with paint thinner will dislodge the gold on an oil-painted surface, but it must be done gently and the thinner must not get on the letters. Latex cleanup can be accomplished using simply a cloth dampened with water.

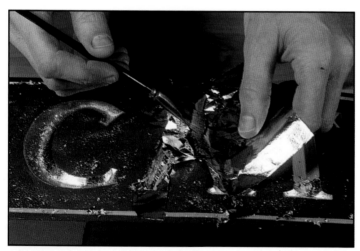

Aluminum leaf is used for special effects such as creating the look of silver because silver leaf tarnishes. Because of its heavier consistency, aluminum can be picked up in the hand, something you cannot do with gold leaf.

GOLD LEAF SUBSTITUTES

Gold leaf is expensive. In the 1990's, the price of gold fluctuated at $350 or more an ounce. Expect to pay a good deal, then, for even a book of gold leaf. Many people think that gold paint is a good substitute for gold leaf at a fraction of the cost. However, even the best brands of gold-leaf paint tend to tarnish outdoors and may turn brown. All gold-leaf paints consist of bronze powder dissolved in lacquer. Imitation gold leaf is available. It comes in sheets that measure 5" by 5"; it too tarnishes quickly outside.

For a special effect, you can purchase aluminum leaf, which is useful wherever a silver color is desired. If you are doing a logo with polished metal parts, a sports motif having skates for example, aluminum leaf is the perfect choice. The material comes in leaves measuring 5" by 5", packed in books of 25 leaves. The cost is nominal.

OUTLINING

Putting an outline around the gold-leafed letters is a way of making them stand out even more. Though black is a popular color for outlining, other colors, depending on the background, enhance the lettering and give a trim appearance.

To outline a letter, use a lettering quill, the same type of brush used to apply gold leaf size. The diameter of the quill will determine the width of the outline. Use a glossy magazine as a palette, as when applying size. Work with small amounts of paint dabbed on the magazine palette.

The key to outlining is keeping a consistently wide line around the letters. This takes concentration and some practice with the quill. It is also easier to outline with an oil paint than a latex because the oil paint flows more smoothly.

For an unusual look called a shadow effect, you can outline just one side of each letter.

If you outline a letter with paint, use a lettering quill.

CHAPTER SEVEN

INSTALLATION AND REPAIRS

Before you even begin to consider installing the sign, you should study where it will be located. Putting a sign inside offers few problems because in most cases it will be protected from the elements, unless it is in direct sunlight; in that case fading will be a problem.

If the sign is to be outdoors, protecting it if possible is important. As it was pointed out earlier, a sign with a southern exposure will deteriorate more quickly than those facing other directions. A sign with a northern exposure, however, may get a buildup of mold, which has to be removed periodically. If a sign is too near a busy road, it becomes the target of dust, dirt, pollution, sand, gravel, salt in snowy climates, and even vandalism. Signs near salt water will quickly deteriorate if not cared for. The more protection offered, the longer the sign will last.

There are any number of ways to display a sign. Mount it on a wall or a single wood or metal post. Install it between posts or suspend it from a bracket. Whatever you decide, there are mounting strategies to follow.

Battens applied to the back of a sign keep it from warping. This batten is being held down with 2½" no. 14 wood screws.

Toggle bolts, lead anchors and galvanized lag screws (l to r) are a sampling of fasteners for mounting signs to posts or buildings.

An assortment of sign screws: galvanized drywall, stainless pan-head, stainless roundhead, machine, bronze, self-tapping masonry, and two brass screws (l to r).

Mounting a sign on a building usually requires ladders. A ladder in the center of a large sign helps support it during the installation process.

BATTENS

Depending upon the exposure and type of wood, wide signs can warp, which means the face of the sign cups inward or outward. Warping is most common in signs made of pine. Redwood is more stable, even in wide panels. To minimize warping, use battens. Battens are boards attached at right angles to the grain. For large signs mounted on an exterior wall, pressure-treated 2x4's work well. Pressure-treated wood has been impregnated with preservatives. The treated 2x4's do not have to be painted and will last for decades. Cedar battens are also recommended. When using 2x4's, drill holes for no. 14 screws or larger, placing them at intervals of 4". Use brass screws because they will not rust. When screwing the battens down, work from one end across the signboard. Make sure the battens are evenly spaced and do not glue them in place. If the sign ever has to be repaired or refinished later on, it will be easier to work on the panel if the battens can be removed. Make sure the screws won't come through any letters.

WALL INSTALLATION

Many signs end up being mounted on walls. Most wood and masonry walls will hold up even the largest signs. For the most secure installation, the best advice to follow is to go heavy on the hardware. It is better to put six screws or bolts into the sign when you think you need only four.

For mounting a typical sign on a wood wall, no. 12 or no. 14 brass screws are ideal. Lag screws, which are similar to threaded screws with a hex head, also work well; use galvanized lag screws for exterior signs. Lag screws thread easily with a ratchet. This is far easier than using a screw driver to install a sign, especially while standing on a ladder. Stainless and bronze fasteners can be used for exterior installation, but they are more expensive than brass. However, they do not rust.

MASONRY WALLS

Much more work is involved when installing a sign on a masonry wall. Drilling into brick or concrete is more difficult than drilling into wood. In fact, you may need a hammer drill, a tool meant exclusively for drilling into brick, concrete or stucco. Hammer drills are rated in terms of blows per minute. The bit, then, actually goes back and forth as it turns.

When installing a sign on a brick or concrete wall, it is better to drill into the mortar than into the brick or concrete. This requires a lot of planning so that the holes in the sign line up with predrilled holes in the mortar. In many cases it is nearly impossible to drill both the sign and the mortar at the same time. Most sign installers use lag screws with lead shields that are inserted into the brick or concrete.

Drilling into a masonry wall using a hammer drill for later sign installation.

WOOD POSTS

Hand-carved wood signs are often mounted on wood posts. The size of the posts will depend on the size of the sign. Realize that a 4x4 post actually measures 3 1/2" by 3 1/2". And a 6x6 measures 5 1/2" by 5 1/2". Redwood and cedar posts are available in 8x8, but they are very expensive.

The best wood for your posts is either cedar or pressure-treated lumber. Construction lumber such as hemlock, fir and spruce will rot out very quickly in the ground. Posts are best set into concrete at a depth of 3' in the ground.

Small signs can be displayed on a single post with a crossarm. The arm is secured by making a lap joint, which means cutting halfway through each member and overlapping them. You can then use carriage bolts to hold them securely to each other.

Post hole diggers are very useful when putting sign posts into the ground.

SPRUCING UP THE POSTS

When you purchase posts, they should be checked over to see that they are warp-free, fairly knot-free and with a minimum of other defects. Sand and finish the posts just as you would the sign panel before putting them into the ground. Another tip is to mark the best face of the post and have that side facing the same

Use a gas-powered drill when no electricity is available. A rachet helps secure sign and post with lag screws.

direction that the sign is oriented. If there are any repairs needed, you can use WEST System®.

Routing the edges of the posts will enhance their appearance. A 4x4 or 6x6 post with squared edges looks unfinished. Use a cove bit or a rounding over bit to take away those sharp corners. Fluting, which means running channels down the faces of the posts, can be done with a straight bit or a round nose bit. Either will create a pleasing effect.

Mount caps on the tops of flat posts for an attractive, finished look. Adding finials, which are wood turnings, on the tops of the caps give an especially decorative look. They can be purchased at fence companies, lumber companies and home centers. Finials are particularly striking when they are gold leafed. Some sign carvers add moldings around the posts. However, these additions tend to encourage water accumulation and wood rot. A simple post with a cap or finial should be sufficient. Most customers of sign carvers prefer to have the posts painted. Though the color varieties are endless, white is the most commonly used color. White is not a distracting color and it complements any color you have chosen for the sign. For cedar, redwood or pressure-treated posts, use at least two or three coats of oil-based primer, then three to four coats of oil or latex paint.

MOUNTING THE SIGN TO THE POSTS

The simplest method for securing a sign to a cross-armed post is with eye bolts. For a different look, suspend the sign with chain, although too much swing may loosen up the hardware causing the sign to come loose. To mount the sign between two posts, use lag screws through the posts and into the edges of the sign. If the sign is thin or you used soft-edged wood like redwood, which may crack when you drill into its edges, use battens on the back of the sign and have the lag screws grip the battens.

Another method for securing a sign between two posts, especially a two-sided sign, is to use dadoes. A dado is basically a groove down the center of a post; the dado allows you to fit the edge of the sign into the groove. To make the

A directory sign. Each sign is mounted between steel straps that are slipped into dadoes or grooves in the posts. The advantage of this type of sign is that it can accommodate changes or deletions of names.

dadoes you need a circular saw, then a chisel to square up the ends of the saw cuts. In addition, secure the sign in place with lag screws through the outside of the posts and into the sign.

METAL BRACKETS AND FASTENERS

Often sign carvers are asked to design a directory sign. This is a sign that has a main panel with additions of names mounted below it. A typical installation is to have metal straps mounted in dadoes cut on the insides of the posts with the different signs edge-mounted to the straps. Mounting is done before the straps are attached to the posts. If a name sign has to be removed or replaced as is often the case, the screws holding the straps in place are removed and the assembly is lifted out of the dadoes. It is then easy to remove a panel. A simpler method is to attach one sign below another with screw eyes and S hooks.

The simplest metal bracket for mounting a sign is a right angle bracket. Sign supply catalogs (see Buyer's Guide) offer brackets that measure as much as 54" long, although smaller ones are available at home centers and hardware stores. The bracket is ideal for small signs that do not need a lot of support.

You can make your own brackets using flat steel or aluminum. To bend the metal you will need a heavy-duty vise. When putting holes into the metals for screws, do the drilling before you do the bending. The best tool for drilling holes in metal is the drill press because you can clamp down the metal to prevent it from spinning out of your hand.

Chains are sometimes used to suspend a sign, but they permit too much movement, especially sideways, which can damage the sign on a windy day. A better suspension technique is to use solid metal supports that also become battens for the back of the sign. Steel or aluminum supports will permit the sign to move back and forth, not sideways.

You can also use flat steel or aluminum to bind the circumference of an oval sign. You will have to secure this metal band to the wood, but the band offers a stronger support than the wood's edge for other fittings that are needed to suspend the sign.

Wrought-iron brackets give a pleasing look to suspended signs.

Assorted brackets called sign shoes, flat mending steel, screw eyes and S hooks are all used for sign installation.

Occasionally signs have to be mounted on roofs. To do this you have to measure the pitch of the roof and make a template that duplicates the roof angle. You can then use flat steel or aluminum to make brackets that conform to the roof pitch.

Professional sign installers may use sign shoes. Basically a right-angle metal bracket made from 1/4" steel, the sign shoe is only available from sign supply catalogs. Sign shoes can be mounted to wood or masonry. Once mounted, the sign is attached to the shoes.

The last resort for acquiring brackets is the blacksmith. Not every community has one, and if you do find a blacksmith, his work is not inexpensive. For ornate brackets that cannot be purchased in stores or through catalogs, the blacksmith is the best resource.

BOAT SIGNS

Attaching a sign to a boat may take some different strategies. Use stainless steel hardware. Brass and bronze screws and bolts tarnish. When mounting a sign on the stern of a boat, it will probably be necessary to put machine screws or bolts through the fiberglass or wood and catch each bolt with a nut on the inside. A piece of wood or small block should back up each bolt on the inside of a fiberglass hull or the fiberglass may crack, or the hole may enlarge. Also be sure to use caulking to prevent leaks.

Bolting a sign will also help bend it if it has to conform to a curved stern. But this is only possible with a signboard that is not too thick and a stern that is only slightly curved. The alternative to getting a wood sign to conform to a curve is to take two thin pieces of wood, bend them in a form, and glue them together. Once the glue is dry the boards will retain the curvature.

LIGHTING A SIGN

One aspect of mounting a sign is having it visible, even at night. The least expensive lighting is the floodlight or spot light. Lighting fixtures can be mounted on a wall, in a roof structure or in the ground. Because direct artificial light tends to wash out the sign at night, make sure the fixtures are as far away from the sign as possible. Fluorescent lighting mounted above or below the sign gives the best illumination, but the fixtures are very expensive.

REPAIRS

After five or ten years, depending on the location, a sign may need some renovation. If it is not in total disrepair, a new coat or two of clear finish or paint may be all that is needed to take away its faded look. If there is mold on the sign because of dampness and lack of direct sunlight, soap and water will usually remove that. A wash-down using soap and water should be done anyway on a yearly basis.

Before refinishing a faded sign, wash it down to remove surface dirt. In most cases, the gold leaf will be intact and will not have to be redone. If a clear finish is coming off and the wood is turning gray, the sign should be sanded down to the bare wood, restained and recoated. If a painted sign is not peeling, paint over it with two or three fresh coats.

Should the gold leaf become scratched, touch it up with new leaf. In fact, gold leaf size can be applied over gold leaf. To shine up the old gold leaf, some sign carvers recommend using cotton dipped in muriatic acid. The trick is to wipe, not rub the gold.

Should an area of the sign deteriorate to the point where there is rot—rare in woods like redwood, mahogany and teak—it is possible to repair it by replacing the rotted wood. This requires some engineering and using WEST System®. The marine epoxy makes for a strong bond and helps fill gaps left when new wood is pieced with old. The epoxy also fills dents and holes in damaged signs.

A badly weathered sign in need of restoration. Outdoor signs, unless refinished every five to ten years, will deteriorate like this one.

You can carve out a crack in a weathered sign with a mill knife and fill the incision with filler or epoxy.

A damaged portion of this sign was routed out and a new piece of wood was epoxied in place.

CHAPTER EIGHT

THE SIGN CARVING PROFESSIONAL

ATTRACTING CUSTOMERS

Although there are many ways to attract customers, the best seems to be word of mouth. Most sign carvers start their careers doing work for family, friends and relatives, and these are the people who will spread the word about the work. The sign carver just starting out may have to be satisfied doing small name and house number signs and boat signs before the large commercial projects come along. The best sign customers seem to be medical doctors, attorneys, dentists, churches, schools and small businesses with an unusual, decorative or collectable product to sell.

ADVERTISING

The telephone book and its yellow advertising pages can generate a lot of business. The best place to have a listing is not under "woodcarving" but under "signs." Although expensive, an advertisement can hold a variety of information about the type of signwork offered. A few lines may suffice. The local newspaper is also a good place to advertise as well as magazines and trade papers. Some sign carvers try to get exposure at craft and trade shows. But the return in commissioned work may be scant.

TRADE WORK

Many sign companies that do plastic, vinyl and metal signs will farm out the wood sign to a sign carver. An advantage to getting jobs this way is that you do not have to deal with the customer directly. The sign company will do the design and even supply the pattern. They will probably do the installation as well. A disadvantage when getting a job from a sign company is that you will probably make less money. It is simply not realistic to charge the same price to the company as you would to the customer.

PRICING SIGNS

To sell your signs, you have to have a formula for pricing the work. Carpenters typically arrive at a price based on the labor and time involved as well as the cost of materials. Sign carvers typically charge by the square foot. How much you charge per square foot depends on the cost of materials and time involved. Materials usually cost from 25 to 33 percent of the job. The square foot formula is an easier one to deal with once you have experience making signs.

It is a good idea when selling your work not to let yourself be compared to another sign carver. You are not selling an automobile. What you are selling is a labor-intensive product that takes a good deal of skill to execute. You need to have the confidence in what you are charging and what you are offering for that price. Your confidence should assure the customer that he is getting a quality sign for a good price.

EDUCATING THE CUSTOMER

The axiom for most businesses is: an educated customer is the best customer. Most sign carvers, however, discover that the typical customer knows little about hand-carved wooden signs. If you want to be a professional sign carver, you have to be willing to explain your work, what skills are involved, and materials such as gold leaf.

As a professional sign carver, you will most likely have to help the customer design the sign. Design elements include lettering styles, carved additions such as logos, and colors. Designing a sign may require that you check out its location to know how big the sign will have to be, where it will best be displayed, and what installation will be necessary. You should also be aware of local building or zoning codes that may dictate how or where a sign may be displayed in proximity to a sidewalk or street.

Some customers ask sign carvers to design logos for them. Logo design is usually not a sign carver's job. He typically works from an existing logo that can come from a business card, stationery, a newspaper ad or a menu.

After the work of on-site evaluation and design, you will have to arrive at an estimate. Estimates are best given on letterhead stationery. You can use transfer letters or a computer to produce a scaled-down drawing that will fit on the stationery. Standard $8^1/_2"$ by 11" paper is best because the size is easy to handle, mail or fax. If you are doing any artwork, the customer should pay a nominal fee. Yet after all the estimating work involved, you may get only half of the jobs for which you gave estimates.

THE PORTFOLIO

Having a portfolio of your work is ideal. It gives the customer an opportunity to see the quality of your work. The portfolio also allows the customer to see what lettering styles are possible, what a carved or appliqued logo will look like, and what sign colors are appealing. You can group the photos by subject—restaurants, lawyers, doctors, houses, boats. Show some in-progress photos of sign making and installation.

MAKING SIGN CARVING A CAREER

Obviously not everyone who has carved a wooden sign successfully will want to choose this for a career or even do it part-time. Materials are costly, the work is labor intensive, a sizeable investment must be made in tools, and the sign carver has to have good business skills. Yet, there are many professional sign carvers who are happy at their work and find an abundance of jobs. There is the reward of putting your product on display and having customers who will enjoy the resulting sign for years to come.

Use a combination of carving techniques to create a unique sign.
The pattern of an egret above was used on the sign for Bull Calf Landing
(page 23). The egret was appliqued and the cattails were v-carved.
The pheasant on this page appears on the author's house sign (page 28).
It was both relief carved and appliqued.

Carved appliques can be used to add interest to a sign. The bison above appears on a sign for Nickels Cafe (page 23).

Appliques of a nautical theme are common additions to signs for seafood restaurants, beach houses and boats. The ship's wheel on this page makes a nice focal point for the Blue Water Yacht Club sign (page 29).

Buyer's Guide

Woodworking Tools

Albert Constantine and Son, Inc.
2050 Eastchester Road
Bronx, New York 10461–2297

Hartville Tool and Supply
940 West Maple St.
Hartville, Ohio 44632
1–800–345–2396

Tools on Sale
Division of 7 Corners Ace Hardware, Inc.
216 West Seventh Street
St. Paul, Minnesota 55102–2599
1–800–328–0457

Woodcraft
210 Wood County Industrial Park
PO Box 1686
Parkersburg, WV 26102–1686
1–800–225–1153

Woodworker's Supply
1108 North Glenn Road
Casper, Wyoming 82601
1–800–645–9292

Woodworkers Warehouse
135 American Legion Hwy
Revere, Massachusetts 02151
1–800–767–9999

Sanding Supplies

Klingspor's Sanding Catalog
PO Box 3737
Hickory, North Carolina 28603–3737
1–800–228–0000

Router Bits

CMT Tools
310 Mears Blvd
Oldsmar, Florida 34677
1–800–531–5559

MLCS Ltd.
P.O. Box 4053 C–17B
Rydal, PA 19046
1–800–533–9298

Gold and Aluminum Leaf Supplies

M. Swift & Sons, Inc.
Ten Love Lane
Hartford, Connecticut 06141–0150
1–800–628–0380

Woodcarving and Woodworking Magazines

American Woodworker
PO Box 7579
Red Oak, Iowa 51591–2579

Chip Chats
National Wood Carvers Association
7424 Miami Ave.
Cinncinnati, OH 45243

CARVING SIGNS - A WOODWORKER'S GUIDE TO CARVING, LETTERING AND GILDING

Fine Woodworking
63 South Main Street
PO Box 5507
Newtown, Connecticut 06470–9871
(800) 888-8286

Sign Builder Illustrated
4905 Pine Cone Dr.
Durham, NC 27707
(800) 638-0776

Sign Business
Box 1416
Broomfield, CO 80020
(303) 469-0424

Sign Update
22 Station Road
Woodford Halse, Northants NN11 3RB
England
44-1327-262621

Sign World
9 West Street
Epsom, Surrey KT18 7RL
England
44-1372-741411

Signcraft
Box 60031
Ft. Myers, FL 33906
(941) 939-4644

Signals
39 Bedford Park Avenue
Richmond Hill, ON L4C 2N9
Canada
(905) 508-7374

Signs of the Times
407 Gilbert Avenue
Cincinnati, OH 45202
(800) 925-1110

Woodcarving Magazine
Castle Place, 166 High St.
Lewes, East Sussex, England BN71XO

Woodshop News
35 Pratt St.
Essex, Connecticut 06426
(860) 767-8227

Woodwork
42 Digital Drive #5
Novato, California 94949

MILL KNIVES

Highland Hardware
1045 N. Highland Ave. NE
Atlanta, Georgia 30306
1–800–241–6748

Lee Valley
12 E. River St.
Ogdensburg, New York 13669
1–800–267–8767

EPOXY

WEST System
Gougeon Brothers, Inc.
P.O. Box 908
Bay City, Michigan 48707
517–684–7286

SIGN SUPPLIES

Dick Blick
P.O. Box 1267
Galesburg, Illinois 61402
1–800–447–8192

N. Glantz & Son
30th Floor
16 Court Street
Brooklyn, New York 11241
718–488–9400